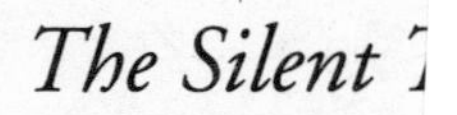

The Silent T

Lost and Found Series

Old Provence by Theodore Andrea Cook
Two Years in the French West Indies by Lafcadio Hearn
The Pilgrimage to Santiago by Edwin Mullins
A Romantic in Spain by Théophile Gautier
The Silent Traveller in London by Chiang Yee
Coming Down the Seine by Robert Gibbings
Journey to Mauritius by Jacques-Henri Bernardin de Saint-Pierre

The Silent Traveller in Oxford

記 畫 津 牛

Chiang Yee

Signal Books
Oxford
2003

This edition published in 2003 by
Signal Books Limited
36 Minster Road
Oxford
OX4 1LY
www.signalbooks.co.uk

First published in 1944

A catalogue record for this book is available from the British Library

ISBN 1-902669-68-1 Cloth
ISBN 1-902669-69-X Paper

Cover Design: Baseline Arts
Typesetting: Devdan Sen
Cover Image: Copyright Bodleian Library, University of Oxford

Printed in Canada

Contents

To Alan

Foreword

ALL MY LIFE I have been pursued by the Silent Traveller, padding steadily after me with his paintbrush and his antique inks.

It was some time in 1941, when my father had packed my mother, my sister, my grandmother and me off to a cottage in Nidderdale, in the Yorkshire Dales, to get away from the bombing, that he brought us a copy of a book called *The Silent Traveller in the Yorkshire Dales.* Being seven at the time, I was less interested in the text than in the pictures. I did know that it was a book by a Chinese gentleman whose name meant "the silent traveller" and who painted the familiar scenes—Kilnsea Crag, a waterfall called Hardraw Force—in a funny Chinese way. I liked the rabbits in Plate IV. I still do. But I was disappointed that the Chinese painter had not thought our dale worth painting.

A few years later, when I was at a boarding school in Oxford, my father presented me with a copy of *The Silent Traveller in Oxford.* This time, he had painted places I passed several times a day, like the Rainbow Bridge in the University Parks. The book became and has remained a favourite. What I didn't know was that at that time Chiang Yee was living in digs less than half a mile from my school.

One day, twenty-five years later, when I was living in New York, I saw what was unmistakably a Silent Traveller watercolour of the lake in Central Park. I was surprised that Chiang Yee had even been to the United States. The bookshop wanted $300 for it, which seemed a lot at the time. I wish I had bought it.

Another quarter of a century on, my wife bought a packet of Christmas cards from the Bodleian Library's gift shop in Oxford with

Chiang Yee's watercolour of the wartime High Street, almost empty except for a red bus, in the snow. One of the friends I sent it to was the then editor of *The Independent on Sunday*. He liked it, and asked me what I knew about the artist. Again, I had no idea that the artist had lived in the very street where I was living in Oxford at the time, Southmoor Road, indeed almost opposite. We lived at number 41; he had lived at 28.

I knew no more about Chiang Yee then than I have just put down. But I rather hoped the editor would ask me to write a piece about him, so I did some research. (In the end the editor was not interested. That is how successful editors become successful, by having just enough enthusiasm to get people to write things, and not enough to over-order.) Here is what I found.

Chiang Yee was born in 1903 in Kiukiang, an old town near the Yangtze in central China famous for selling the porcelain that is made nearby. His real name was Chiang Chung-ya. The family were not rich, but they were what our forefathers would have called "gentry". They claimed descent from an emperor who had lived in the second millennium BC, and they had owned certain lands, both rich "waterfields" and rougher "mountain fields", since the tenth century, which would make all British dukes parvenus by comparison. In all that time neither the tenant families nor the rents they paid had changed much. The extended Chiang family shared a sprawling home called "the house of the three footpaths".

Chung-ya's mother died when he was five, shortly before the revolution of 1912 and the Japanese invasion destroyed a way of life that had lasted with only slow change over many centuries. In 1940, seven years after he left China, Chiang Yee (let us give him the name he chose for himself) recalled the immemorial customs, the festivals and the feeling of growing up in that traditional home in an elegiac book, *A Chinese Childhood*, full of warmth and affection, but tinged with the sorrow and sometimes with the bitterness of exile.

As was by then his habit, he illustrated his own book with his own watercolours and line drawings. It was an appropriate tribute, for his father, Chiang Ho-an, was a painter. Chiang Yee remembered how, once he was twelve, he was allowed to mix pigments and to make willow-charcoal for rough sketches. He learned how his father painted flowers and butterflies by watching them carefully for a long time. Perhaps that early training explains why, as it seems to me, when he painted those subjects (or the rabbits in the Dales) his work was more conventional, more "Chinese", than when he painted figures, portraits, or—his special *forte*—landscape.

He studied chemistry, "for some reason", at the National South Eastern University in Nanking. After doing military service and brief spells teaching chemistry and then as a journalist, he became the District Governor of four districts, including Kiukiang, which he found a "tiresome talking job". Probably that is why for his writing and painting he chose the pen-name of *Yah Hsin-che*, which means "dumb-walking man", or, more elegantly, "Silent Traveller".

For a while in 1932 he lived on a houseboat on Lake Tai in Soochow. In 1933, apparently after an argument with the local warlord, a disagreement that, given the habits of the warlords of the time, might have proved fatal, he left for England. That was the natural place to go, because Kiukiang had been a British "treaty port", and the British, if not particularly popular, were at least a known evil. Chiang Yee and a young relative set out on a French boat from Shanghai to Marseille, knowing virtually no word of either French or English between them. Chiang Yee left behind a wife and four children. (The warlord must have been genuinely lethal.) The wife and daughters stayed in China. The two sons found their way to the West much later, one to the United States, and one to Britain.

After one night in Paris, he came to London, where, in spite of the fact that it was the depths of the Depression, Chiang Yee soon found work. He began by teaching Chinese at the School of Oriental and African Studies, and in 1938 went to work as a consultant to the Wellcome Museum of the History of Medicine, now merged into the Science Museum.

Chiang Yee was born at the foot of Lu Mountain, one of the most famous mountains in China, so in his very first summer in England he lifted his eyes up unto the hills. He joined a party of holidaymakers who were heading for Snowdonia. The next summer he went to the Lake District, It was on the evening of July 31, 1936 that he reached Wasdale

Head. It was the Lake District that he made the subject of his first book. When he had finished the text and the watercolours, he sent it off hopefully to a publisher, then to several others. The response was depressing, not least for its stupidity. The publisher wrote back that the drawings were so utterly Chinese that no one in England would understand them. And the book would find very few readers. Methuen, however, thought differently, and in 1938 *A Silent Traveller in the Lake District* duly appeared.

Even before that, only two years after he had arrived in London, his first book, *The Chinese Eye*, had been published. It is a fairly astonishing product from a man who had been using English for less than two years, even though, as he generously conceded in his acknowledgment, he was helped both by his friend the playwright S.I. Hsiung and by Miss Innes Jackson, who "rendered into lucid English my clumsy expressions."

China, of course, was in the news in the 1930s. British intellectuals watched in fascination the Chinese Revolution, the Long March, the Japanese invasion, the Rape of Nanking and the Hoang Ho floods. There was a big exhibition of Chinese art at Burlington House in 1935. *The Chinese Eye* was an overnight success. (It was reprinted within a month.) Before long Chiang Yee had made an amazing variety of friends. They included George Bernard Shaw; the Yorkshire squire Sir William Middleton, who invited him to stay at Parcevall Hall, where he wrote *The Silent Traveller in the Yorkshire Dales*; Edward, Lord Longford, brother of the more famous Frank and angel of the Gate Theatre in Dublin; and Laurence Binyon, Keeper of Chinese books at the British Museum. A particular friend he met at the Burlington House show was A.D. Brankstone, a young scholar in the Chinese department of the British Museum who went to China for the Ministry of Information and the British Council during the war, fell ill and died in Hong Kong.

His acquaintances included assorted dons, art experts and even ballet dancers. Ninette de Valois invited him to do the décor and costumes for a Sadler's Wells ballet, *The Birds*, so he met the great Australian dancer Robert Helpmann and the young Beryl Grey. He was obviously not above what used to be called "lion hunting". He describes how he struck up acquaintance with such eminent figures of the day as Sir William Beveridge, father of the National Health Service, and the classicist and

League of Nations supporter Sir Gilbert Murray, as well as Sir Arthur Evans, the excavator of Knossos, who allowed Chiang Yee to paint in the grounds of his mansion, Youlbury, on Boar's Hill outside Oxford. But to be fair, he was a very interesting man himself, as well as a charming one, and something of a Chinese lion at a time when Republican China was an ally, but a very unknown one.

Although he was trained as a chemist, he was astonishingly well-read in both Chinese and English literature. He quotes easily from Shelley, Wordsworth and Richard Jefferies, as well as from the Chinese classics.

What gives his writing its special charm for me is a certain deadpan way of looking at Western ways of doing things from a point of view at once utterly clued up (he never makes a mistake about, for example, Oxford slang or Edinburgh dialect) and at the same time utterly foreign. He notices British class arrogance and racial conceit and puts them gently in their place as from the great height of a gentleman born into a very old and very confident civilization. Here he is at the Oxford Union, for example. "While my friend and I were having tea, a huge square figure in a black coat suddenly stood up in a corner of the room, stretched out his arm dramatically towards the servant and said, 'I want some salt—salt!' He was undoubtedly an Oxford graduate who knew the place and the servant so well that formality was superfluous." The irony is not less biting for being so gentle.

He moved to Oxford after his digs in London were bombed and stayed there for five years. Immediately after the war, he spent a few months in the United States, then returned to Oxford. But in 1955 he emigrated to America, where he taught Chinese language and culture at Columbia University in New York for the next 16 years, with stints at Harvard and the Australian National University to prove his growing academic eminence. The Silent Traveller still found time to add Paris and Dublin, a wonderful portrait of Boston and San Francisco to his portfolio of travels.

The books are much more than illustrated travel guides. They are the pretext for a stream of anecdote, comparison and sometimes quite sharp comment on the mores and self-images of the people he meets, especially at the slightest hint of complacency or colonial superiority. But it is the illustrations that give them their special quality for me.

Chiang Yee was the master of three distinct styles: precise line drawings, often with a deft touch of gentle caricature; black-and-white water colours, like the powerful, rain-washed townscapes of Edinburgh or the early views of the Lake District; and his delicate, full colour water colours, like those of Oxford and Boston and especially of his childhood.

His technique was always influenced by the brushstrokes of Chinese calligraphy. But he was irritated by those who saw his work as typically Chinese. "The results are not Chinese in any typical sense", he wrote. "They are the personal impressions of one Chinese, not of all Chinese."

After the "Nixon shock" of 1972 and the reopening of China, he went home and his last book was called *China Revisited after Forty-Two Years.* Probably, like his eminent Chinese contemporary in America, the architect I. M. Pei told me of himself, he never stopped feeling Chinese at heart. He returned to China for a long visit in 1977 and died there in October that year. The Polish-born writer Evan Hoffman, taken to Canada as a child and educated in the United States, has brilliantly described the emotional complexities of emigration in her book *Lost in Translation.* Chiang Yee was never lost, but then he was never translated. He used his Chinese technique but also a Chinese sensibility to create works that are neither Chinese nor Western, but universal in sympathy and profoundly humane.

Godfrey Hodgson
Oxford, 2003

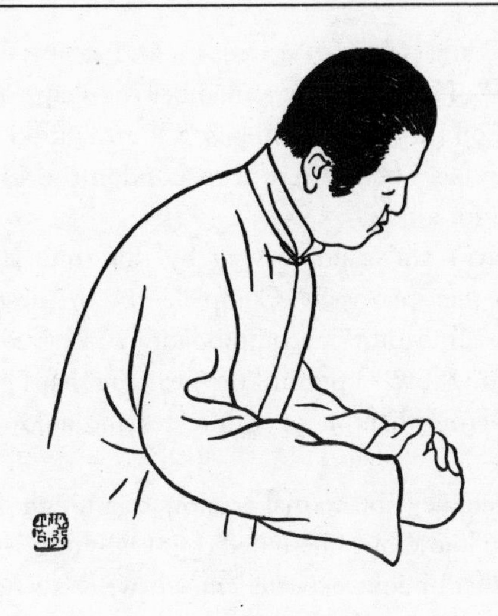

1
The First Bow

WHEN I was a child my elders used to tell me smilingly that whenever I approached the gate of a new city wall I must bow to it before I passed through. I imagined that this was intended to be a sign of respect to a strange place and an expression of the hope of making its acquaintance—perhaps also a propitiatory gesture, for we Chinese think that those who hold their heads high may lower them a little if we pay them our respect first.

It was inevitable that this custom should come to mind when I visited Oxford for the first time, for we Chinese value learning very highly, and Oxford is noted throughout the world as a city of learning. I gave it my first bow in 1934, when I spent ten days or so there. During that short time I was taken by friends from one college to another, from one old building to another.

Time passed, and when I visited Oxford again on a very wet afternoon in 1937, I could hardly remember the shape of any of them. I had been asked on this occasion to give a short talk on Chinese Art at Rhodes House and as I had to return to London the same night there was scarcely time for a bow.

And now here I am again, having by this time already lived in Oxford for more than two years. Compelled by the destruction of my London rooms to find other accommodation, I arrived in Oxford in rather a turmoil, and it was not until the next day that I gave it the deep bow it deserved. From then on I began to see and enjoy the city in my own way.

It is my unalterable habit to make a note or a rough sketch of places I visit and learn to know, but I hesitated over Oxford. Friends who know my "Silent Traveller" books expected me to write also about Oxford; some were kind enough to suggest the names of people with whom I should get into touch, and even which scenes I should paint. But things did not work out so easily. I came to Oxford in war-time, when many of the colleges are closed to visitors, and as I am not a member of any college I cannot rank myself with the Tuft-hunters—if indeed there *are* any Tufts or noblemen here now. I have tried to make the acquaintance of old college servants in the hope of hearing amusing anecdotes, but they are apt to be reserved nowadays when dealing with foreigners. After all, I sometimes tell myself, so many books have been written about Oxford that it would be unwise for me to invite comparison with them and to face the criticism of Oxford scholars by writing another. So I have remained silent.

But life is too short and precious for us to pass through it without leaving a few footprints behind us. A man's experience in a certain place at a certain time must be unique, in some way different from the experience of others. Why should I not leave a few words to mark one period in my brief life? Even a bird's clawprints remain for a little time in the snow. Let these impressions of my short years in Oxford remain as long.

December 1942

2
"Shall I Climb over the Wall?"

"SHALL I climb over the wall?" I asked when my friend Ni Tao-hsi questioned my ability to find a way out of Wadham College at about half-past twelve one night. I had not realized that I had stayed so long, and there I was without even having found a place to sleep.

I had arrived in Oxford that day to escape from the strain of the fierce London blitzes (October 1940). Luckily I knew Tao-hsi and had sent him a wire that morning. I call him by his christian name Tao-hsi, but he is known to his English friends as Christopher Ni, or Jimmy Ni. He took me to his rooms in the college to rest while he went out to keep an appointment, promising to find me somewhere to stay on his way.

Shall I climb over the wall?

When he came back he did not say what success he had had, being apparently too depressed at not being able to take me to dinner in Hall as his guest owing to wartime food restrictions. A restaurant seemed the only alternative, and he suggested taking me to the Mitre or the Randolph; but we were both tired and ultimately Tao-hsi decided to cook some spaghetti over the fire. I do not know how he managed it, but it was very good.

He had to go out again after the meal. In the interval I learned something about his college life. The rooms he occupied belonged to a college don who had been called up for military service; Tao-hsi was allowed to use them for the whole term by paying a little extra to the college authorities.

After my friend had gone out I started to examine the rooms. I was in the biggest, which I presumed was the room in which the tutor entertained his friends and the undergraduates under his supervision. It had two big windows, one facing the quadrangle and the other the garden. Before a large fire-place were a comfortable sofa and two armchairs. I sat in a swivel chair at a writing-desk and imagined the tutor turning to question his pupils. A door near the window facing the garden led to the bedroom, which, though small, was very cosy and neat, well lit by a window also facing the garden, and warmed by a small electric fire. Near the other window in the sitting-room was a tiny room with many varied bottles, glasses, plates and dishes arranged on the shelves, and two or three cupboards. Opposite the bedroom was a study full of books which Tao-hsi was not allowed to use.

I was busily engaged in thinking of the kind of life the tutor must be leading in the army as compared with his former life in these rooms, when I was interrupted by the arrival of two servants, each carrying a dozen bottles of beer. They took no notice of me. One remarked that Mr. Ni was entertaining his friends again. When they had gone, leaving the beer, a third entered with ten or more bottles of mineral water. I wondered whether Tao-hsi always bought drinks in such quantity, especially since he had plenty in his cupboard. Boxes of cigarettes and pastries were then brought.

I sat in silence until an elderly tailor came in, with two new suits in his arms. He was talkative and asked if I knew where Mr. Ni was, saying that he always tried to catch Mr. Ni in the evenings as he could not get hold of him at any other time. He liked Mr. Ni very much; Mr. Ni was a nice scholar to serve; in fact, he had served Mr. Ni for nearly two years now. I remembered having read in *Recollections of Oxford*, by G. V. Cox, that "the Oxford tradesmen's system of 'giving credit' and their notorious anxiety to get a young man's name on their books had then, as now, their usual effect on thoughtless youths, who were thus entrapped and, for want of funds, could not extricate themselves." Tao-hsi, however, was not a "thoughtless youth", and so far as I knew had not found it impossible to "extricate" himself; moreover, this tailor certainly did not look like a dun.

Conversation

At length the tailor grew tired of waiting, gathered up the suits, and left a message that Mr. Ni should try them on at his shop. I persuaded him, however, to stay a little longer, and tell me any stories he knew of Wadham College. It appeared that he knew plenty, and was nothing loth to relate them to a sympathetic listener. He declared that a ghost had once inhabited the room just opposite Tao-hsi's, a ghost who used to tramp up and down the stairs at night. Nobody knew who it was or what it was doing. "We have heard nothing of him for some time now," the tailor concluded.

Some time after the tailor's departure, there came into the room a friend of Tao-hsi's, whom he had invited for the evening. We did not introduce ourselves, for it seemed that such formality was hardly necessary, inside the college rooms. Though I was an outsider and not acquainted with the fashionable topics of conversation among undergraduates, we succeeded in keeping each other interested while we were waiting. This young fellow was evidently familiar with Tao-hsi's rooms and soon busied himself with a bottle of beer and glasses. I told him I seldom drank. Then he helped himself to a cigarette.

Tao-hsi and his friends shortly streamed in, and the guests promptly began to drink and smoke without waiting to be asked, for Tao-hsi preferred them to do as they liked. Soon the room was filled with noise and high-pitched voices. I could not make head or tail of the conversation. The sentences seemed short and unfinished, and there was much shouting of names, and the wireless was on. I had a small glass of sherry and felt my face growing warm as I sat smiling through the clamour.

A young man called Roger Crosskey, who could not have been more than twenty, was sitting on one of the arms of my chair. When he discovered that I was the only person without a cigarette he remarked smilingly that I was a very good "young" lad. His youthful glowing face made me forget that I was certainly double his age. Another young fellow, about the same age as Roger, became for a time more or less the centre of the conversation. I learnt that he had just taken the part of "Bimbo" in Ian Hay's play, "The Housemaster", which had run in the Oxford Playhouse for about a week. He wore a pair of red-brown corduroy trousers, the brightness of which made him look the youngest in the room, and his mobile, mischievous face suggested a very promising actor.

Occasionally came a loud and rather harsh laugh from a South African, the cheeriest person in the room. He had been standing by the fire-place all the time with a big glass in one hand and a bottle in the other, not talking much and only moving now and then to fetch another bottle. The rest of us watched and laughed at him, and he laughed back more loudly each time. I remember counting as many as five bottles, but he never stopped drinking. What an admirable character he must have had to be able to enjoy the laughs against him!

I do not know how the talk came round to honesty. A slim young fellow with a pale face and elegant figure roused himself from the sofa and told us a story of the most honest man of Wadham College, of whom A. J. C. Hare wrote in *The Story of My Life* :

> *I breakfasted the other day at Wadham with a most extraordinary man called R., whose arms and legs all straggle away from his body, and who holds up his hands like a kangaroo. His oddities are a great amusement to his friends, who nevertheless esteem him. One day a man said to him, "How do you do, R.?" and he answered, "Quite well, thank you". Imagine the man's astonishment at receiving next day a note— "Dear Sir, I am sorry to tell you that I have been acting a deceptive part. When I told you yesterday that I was quite well, I had really a headache: this has been upon my conscience ever since." The man was extremely amused, and showed the letter to a friend, who, knowing R.'s frailties, said to him, "Oh, R., how could you act so wrongly as to call Mr. Burton 'Dear Sir'—thereby giving him the impression that you liked him, when you know that you dislike him extremely?" So poor R. was sadly distressed, and a few days later Mr. Burton received the following: "Burton, I am sorry to trouble you again, but I have been shown that, under the mask of friendship, I have been for the second time deceiving you: by calling you dear sir, I may have led you to suppose that I like you, which I never did, and never can do. I am, Burton, Yours &c."!* [1]

Though he did not quote the above verbatim, the manner of the story-teller lent effect to the story, and we all enjoyed it.

There was another man in the party, rather older than the others—I forget whether he was a Hungarian or a Czech—who seemed to have a fund of stories to tell. With an English pipe in his hand, he poured out one story after the other, while continually brandishing the pipe, knocking out the ashes, and filling it with fresh tobacco. He was a very experienced story-teller, and at the end of each story there was general laughter. The South African laughed too, even though he now held the bottle to his mouth instead of the glass.

None of us heeded the time, for we were all absorbed in the stories. Towards the end of the evening the jokes became broader. I recollected that during my own college days in China whenever a number of students were gathered together, the talking and joking always finally came round to what in England are called "smokeroom topics". I do not think there is cause for concern in this. Confucianists have continually tried severely to suppress such subjects, but without avail. Century after century the "naughty" themes recur. Human beings, I reflected—not by any means for the first time—have the same inner nature in all parts of the world, though they may differ outwardly in face, dress, and language.

At last some one suggested bed. Discovering with alarm that it was half-past twelve, I recalled that I had no idea where I could spend the night. Tao-hsi proposed that, unless I preferred to climb over the college wall, I should sleep on his sofa. Before I could make up my mind the undergraduates kindly produced some blankets and the question was settled. The guests then dispersed, the South African being the last to go because he wanted to empty all the bottles. There was still loud laughter when they were out in the quadrangle, then all was quiet. The sudden hush after such a clamour gave me a shivery feeling for a moment.

A faint snoring soon issued from Tao-hsi's room, and I curled myself up on the sofa. But I could not sleep. The events of the evening passed through my mind again like a film show, and I remembered particularly what the old tailor had told me. Putting on my coat over my pyjamas I went stealthily downstairs. It was too dark to see anything, and the beautiful Wren buildings of Wadham College had lost their contours completely in the blackest sky I had ever faced. I was soon driven back by the biting wind in the quadrangle, to roll myself up again on the sofa. An amusing thought struck me that though I had tried not to make a noise as I went down, the wooden staircase must have creaked a little under my weight. If the undergraduates in the rooms nearby were still awake, they must have thought they had heard that long-forgotten ghost tramping the stairs again. Whether they were frightened or excited at the experience I did not want to know: I felt excited myself at having, for once, *been* a ghost!

[1] Quoted from Lewis and Fenby's *Anatomy of Oxford* (Jonathan Cape).

3
What Do I Know of Shelley?

RAIN fell heavily as I came out of the quiet Queen's Lane into the High. Young men were streaming up the steps and entering a venerable building almost immediately opposite Queen's College. I followed them. No one stopped or questioned me; indeed, no one heeded me at all. I did not know that this was University College until, mingling with the young men, I read the notices on the board hanging by the porter's room. (I had not long been in Oxford then.) Suitcases and trunks lay about, flat or up-ended, and some of the young men appeared jolly and self-possessed, while others looked self-conscious or nervous. It was the first term of the university year.

Two freshmen

Presently the young men scattered. I followed two of them along a darkish passage, which grew steadily darker until I emerged into a spacious hollow place through the domed roof of which a dim light penetrated, and I saw the Shelley Memorial for the first time. The two young fellows immediately ahead of me did not stop but turned up a staircase and entered a room. From the remark one of them made: "Have you read much Shelley?" I concluded that they were freshmen, for if they had been there before they would probably not even have mentioned Shelley as they passed.

I was left standing by the railings alone.

Here lay the image of the great English poet. Though the sculpture depicts his body as it was washed ashore, he looks very peaceful. No doubt it is a good piece of work, but the dim surroundings, though they enhance the peace, create a feeling of rather dead sadness which might, I thought, be justified if it hung over the poet's tomb in Italy, but which appear unduly cold in a memorial. I have no idea how the monument was planned, but it struck me as illustrating some lines in one of Shelley's own poems:

And like a dying lady, lean and pale,
Who totters forth, wrapped in a gauzy veil,
Out of her chamber, led by the insane
And feeble wanderings of her fading brain,
The moon arose up in the murky East,
A white and shapeless mass—

Perhaps the sculptor had these lines in mind… However that may be, the memorial gave me a different impression of Shelley from the one I had previously entertained. Certainly he possessed an elegant, even feminine, body, but, too, he had a brave heart which dared to express what others dared not mention.

But what, after all, do I really know of Shelley? I am no student of the world's literatures, and in my boyhood in China, and even in my college life, during which for some reason I studied chemistry, his name did not occur. It was not until I had finished my university education a few years later that I picked up a small book in a friend's house and found in it a translation of a poem by Shelley. The feeling of the poem seemed to me akin to that which is to be found in many Chinese poems. The translation was in the Chinese classical style, and the translator was himself a gifted poet, so it is probable that my enjoyment was of the language of the translation rather than of the meaning of the original, for I was at that time not competent to judge the faithfulness of a translation. I have forgotten the title of the piece now. As opportunity arose I read other translations of Shelley done into modern Chinese, that is to say in free verse without rhyme or regular metre. I enjoyed these too, but I do not believe that the poetry of a language is truly translatable into any other language, and I was glad when I could read Shelley in the original. I'm afraid I do not understand many of his poems. I enjoy most of his lyrics and odes, though even these I can never hope to understand as completely as the English understand them. It does not matter to me so long as my heart responds as far as it is able to what I read. Poetry speaks to the human heart, our philosophers say, and my humble thought on reading Shelley's poems is that he had a full understanding of the human heart and life. He wrote:

I dare not guess; but in this life
Of error, ignorance, and strife,
Where nothing is, but all things seem
And we the shadows of the dream,

It is a modest creed, and yet
Pleasant if one considers it,
To own that death itself must be,
Like all the rest, a mockery.

That garden sweet, that lady fair,
And all sweet shapes and odours there,
In truth have never passed away:
'Tis we, 'tis ours, are changed; not they.

For love, and beauty, and delight,
There is no death nor change: their might
Exceeds our organs, which endure
No light, being themselves obscure.

He shed tears on a faded violet, whereas most human beings refuse to dwell upon the sad and unpleasant things of life; it is not that they have no knowledge of them. Again, he wrote:

Oh, cease! must hate and death return?
Cease! must men kill and die?
Cease! drain not to its dregs the urn
Of bitter prophecy.

The world is weary of the past,
Oh, might it die or rest at last!

Does this not express what we all, or at least most, of us want to say just now? This, I think, could be used as a guiding star for the peace conference which must follow the present horrible war.

Since seeing the Shelley Memorial I have tried to find out a little more about Shelley. In his lifetime he seems always to have been misunderstood. At Eton he gained the nickname of "Mad Shelley". He was condemned and expelled from University College for publishing *The Necessity of Atheism,* which attacked conventional theology. His first wife, Harriet Hitchener, was incapable of understanding him. English traditional thought and law gave him no support in his ill-health and financial difficulties. The English judges at that time did not even allow him to have the custody of his own children, for they thought that he was unfitted to bring them up. Often in poverty and sorrow, he was an exile from England. How sad and strange that a humane and understanding creature like Shelley should meet such adverse fortunes! No law or single rule can be applied to all men. Shelley was only one of many in like case.

There is, however, something everlasting in the law of truth. Had not Shelley truthfully given expression to his real human feelings he might have remained unknown. I think it is a testimony to the admirable English capacity for correcting their faults that the Shelley Memorial was erected in the college from which he was expelled or, as Shelley himself put it, where he received "unworthy treatment".

In China poets and artists have always been regarded as either fools or madmen, as beings generally not worth speaking of, bad tempered, with peculiar habits and no knowledge of how to live—until they were dead. The general mass of my country thinks that poets and artists should behave like the general mass, forgetting that the general mass is a somewhat shabby mixture of drunkenness, vanity, wealth, rigid tradition, and sophisticated manifestation of the fallibility of human laws. They cannot see themselves for what they are. Perhaps poets and artists have clearer and fresher minds. Being myself a poet and artist in a small way, quite without expectation of achieving anything, even I have often been pointed to by some of my fellow-countrymen as a "victim" of the Muses. But I really do not mind being misunderstood so long as I do not understand others.

I, a humble Chinese, do not know the English general mass. However, had Shelley lived today he might have led a very different life. I wonder how he would have behaved at receptions and parties, and how he would have answered his fan mail? We have a saying, "Good poems can be written in the bitterest life"; and perhaps Shelley is an outstanding example of the truth of this saying. He wrote that death itself must be a mockery. I think that it is life which is the mockery.

I have a personal feeling for the name Shelley. A compatriot and friend of mine, Wang Li-hsi, who had a great passion for the poet's work, chose Shelley for his English first name. (Like all Chinese he had a Chinese "first" name, but, like some, he preferred to be known by an English first name among his many English friends.) He was Professor Shelley Wang. He came to live in this country only a month before I did, but he subsequently travelled far and wide in Europe as I have not. Politically he was strongly revolutionary. We actually shared a flat in London for a year, and as we met then nearly every day, the name Shelley came to ring in my ears. Once about a trivial matter I told him that he had misunderstood me. He answered that he had always tried to understand others and that he had never intentionally misunderstood any one. His life was not unlike Shelley's. In his younger days he was expelled from school; his first wife did not understand him; very many Chinese rejected his ideas for the social reconstruction of their country; he wrote good poetry in Chinese classical styles as well as in free verse; he was often in poverty and sorrow, and his residences in Europe were periods of exile. He once wrote:

How is one worth a bowl of rice by selling writings?
Endangered by life yet craving to live I left my country
But history has always been made by swords and guns,
Those fighting on paper nothing but dogs and horses—
The huntsman hallos them on.

(Translated by Miss Sylvia Townsend Warner.)

Again, on Lake Annecy, in Switzerland:

Tenderly like the hand of a mother
The lake wind smoothes my face.
Far have I travelled—but nowhere
Have found a more enchanting scenery than this.
Mont Blanc's turret of ice
Has rung its changes of beauty for millions of years:
At noon it is like a transparent blue stone
And cannot be distinguished from the sky and water;
The setting sun gives it new colours,
It glitters with every shade of red and purple.
Peace is the heart of the universe,
Beauty is given in wedlock to the soul of man,
But now
We in our world are water
Grumbling, quarrelling, and wrestling in a boiling cauldron.

(Translated by Miss Sylvia Townsend Warner.)

When China was invaded by the Japanese, many Chinese in Europe tried to get back to their loved country. Shelley Wang eventually succeeded, in 1938. It is more than two years now since the news reached me of his death at the front— just after I had received a copy of his last volume of poems entitled *Exile and Wars.* He did not devote all his energy to writing poetry, and I cannot now foresee his name being remembered a hundred years hence. But I could not fail to be deeply moved by the recollection of him as I stood before the Shelley Memorial.

4
Mixed Feelings

ONE of the differences between Oxford and London is the atmosphere of the bookshops and the conversation of their customers. The feeling inside Oxford bookshops is one of the most striking features of the city.

It so happened that the first of them with which I became acquainted was Mowbray's, by the entrance to Oxford market. It sells chiefly religious books, and each time I am there I see, dodging from shelf to shelf, one or two elderly—if not really old—men in black gowns. Such black-clad persons are abundant in Oxford; but I am not interested in their clothes so much as in the things they wear on their heads, some of which are square, some small and round, some round with a wide brim. If I were to write and tell some of my compatriots who have never been abroad that in England I had seen priests walking round the market, I do not know what they would think, because our priests, at any rate the Buddhist ones, if not the Taoist, are not supposed to eat meat, and consequently must not frequent markets, as that would suggest that they were fond of food rather than of their work. But these Oxford priests, I should have to explain, go to the market to buy mental food.

By rights, surely, the centre for all students and bookworms in Oxford should be the showroom or sales department of the Oxford University Press. But this is not so, though in the windows of the building are to be seen many of the Press's publications arranged neatly on shelves. The Manager and assistants always remind me (I hope they

Some of the people in black

will not mind my saying so) of those elegantly-dressed elderly butlers that I have met in some of the great houses of England. I feel that I ought not only to pay respect to the antique flavour of the furniture in such places, but behave with all circumspection to the butlers. Why should the faces of these men always look so controlled and expressionless? Perhaps I should not ask such a question, for we Chinese are supposed to be emotionless creatures ourselves. Anyhow, it is no wonder that "untouchable" undergraduates and shabby bookworms like me do not often come that way. I must not neglect to mention how great is the name of the Oxford University Press; I knew it before I came to England, and I was told that any book published by this Press was a standard one. How, therefore, could I miss paying it a visit now that I was in Oxford? I visited also the Clarendon Press in Walton Street.

The best spot in which to see typical Oxford characters is the neighbourhood of Broad Street and Holywell Street. In peace-time they may be conspicuous in other parts of Oxford, but now it is only here that one notices these fancifully-dressed undergraduates, the white-haired professors, the scholarly-looking men and women. At Carfax and in the main streets round it they are lost in the crowd of war-time residents. There are several reasons why these traditional Oxford figures

Two undergraduates in Broad Street

Port Meadow in snow

frequent this neighbourhood. Here are situated many colleges and the Bodleian Library: but the main attraction is the two big bookshops, Blackwell's and Parker's. I may be wrong, but I think Blackwell's is generally the first choice, and those who cannot get in go to Parker's. I have not made many friends in Oxford yet, but already I have often heard people say: "I will order it from Blackwell's," or "I shall consult Blackwell." It seems to me rather unfair that Blackwell's should always have priority. I cannot myself afford to spend much money on books, but I always feel inclined to give my custom, such as it is, to the smaller shops. Probably the manager of Blackwell's does not miss my orders, as I make only small purchases. I do, however, like to look round Blackwell's from time to time. Why should this shop attract so many visitors? It must be by good management and the attractive manner in which the books are displayed.

I shall always remember my first visit there, soon after I came to Oxford. It was about mid-term, in November 1940. Crossing Beaumont Street and passing the Martyrs' Memorial, I walked along the wall of Balliol College to Broad Street. An old professor in a long black gown with a small square-topped cap under his right arm was coming out of a doorway next to the entrance of the college. His eyes were fixed on his feet; but the approach of another white-bearded person in an ordinary suit with an umbrella in his hand caused him to lift his head. They exchanged remarks on the increasing coldness of the weather. I could still see a few yellow leaves lying on the pavement, fallen from the trees inside the gateway of Trinity College.

A corner of Balliol

A notice "Closed to Visitors" hanging at the entrance to Balliol College prevented me from looking inside, so I went to have a look at the beautiful lawn of Trinity College with its many well-shaped trees. I remembered having heard that Trinity is now the only college which does not admit Orientals. My flat face could not be disguised, so I passed on without entering to avoid misunderstandings. Four undergraduates were walking ahead of me. They were all very young, and had brightly coloured woollen scarves wound round their necks so many times that they looked like human giraffes. Two of them did not as yet look like typical Oxford undergraduates, but the other two had the familiar up-and-down movement of the shoulders. Three more came towards me with scarves worn in the same way. They reminded me of a certain type of young Burmese girl who lengthens her neck with copper rings as a means of beautifying herself. I wish I could get hold of a few of these long-necked undergraduates for a display in China after the war!

Human giraffe

I followed both groups into Blackwell's. It was crowded. Some of the girl undergraduates had their worn-out black jackets on their shoulders, and I wondered why they did not have new ones to match their clothes. I sauntered from one room to another. Peeping over somebody's shoulder I noticed that he had just picked up the only visible copy of my little book *The Silent Traveller in the Yorkshire Dales.* This naturally roused my interest, but I did not know whether to be pleased or not, for the customer had not yet bought the book. In the next few minutes I was somehow driven right to the back of the shop. An elderly man, when I came to his corner, lowered his head and buried himself in his book, and soon I heard him snoring.

I had a quick look round at the beautifully bound second-hand books upstairs, then came down and entered a small room full of children's books. A lady visitor was telling a little girl to amuse herself with the many illustrated books until she returned from shopping in the market. How kind of the manager of Blackwell's to provide this nursery!

When I came out of the juvenile room I saw the only copy of my little book again, still there. I sighed. Presently two elderly ladies moved up to the table where it was lying. I tried not to watch them, but before very long I overheard one say that she had read my *Silent Traveller in London.* "It was quite amusing," she said, "to read the Chinaman's view of our capital, but he does not seem very silent to me."—"Oh, I must read it then," said the other. I was interested to learn that the other lady wanted to read my book because my writing was not consistent with my name, but perhaps she did not mean it quite in that way. I took another walk round, and when I came back the book was still there! I sighed again, wondering why I could not control myself and was so easily touched by such an unimportant event. Not every book can be sold day after day, and not every one can, or would want to, buy my book. Those who had looked at it may have found it not quite to their taste, or may not have wanted to spend money in these hard times. I ought not really to mind whether they bought it or not. But this is too theoretical! The greengrocer does not like to see his greens remain in his shop; and no mother will admit that her baby is not pretty. I know vanity is a great handicap to human nature, but I would have just liked to feel that my book had attracted another reader, no matter whether he enjoyed it or not. Still, the crowd in the shop would not be interested in my feelings, and in any case they probably did not know that I was the humble author of that insignificant little book. The only way to control my partial feelings was to leave Blackwell's.

I proceeded to Parker's. I bought a set of six volumes of Morris's *British Birds,* published in 1870, with many hand-coloured illustrations, bound in half-polished olive Levant morocco "extra". When I asked the shop assistant to send the books to my address, he smiled at me and said he had been selling a good many copies of my books. Where now was the justification for my disappointment? I returned his smile.

It is better to live one's life without these mixed feelings!

5
An Ivory Model

MANY scenes have become familiar since I came to Oxford. In winter I have often watched the old coalman bending under a heavy sack and mounting the doorsteps with great care, while from his nostrils and mouth is ejected a white vapour which spreads in a halo round his red face. After delivering coal at one house he goes next door. His patient horse occasionally lifts its hooves and stamps noiselessly upon the snow to warm itself. Sometimes I have seen housewives complaining that the coalman is late again, and wondering whether they will get their weekly ration of coal. Sometimes I have watched a middle-aged woman, carrying a tiny baby wrapped in a bright ragged shawl, going from door to door to sell the logs which her husband is bringing in his horse-drawn cart. The housewife, if she already has enough logs, seldom answers the door, and the woman proceeds wearily to the next house.

Log seller

Shelley might have been thinking of Oxford in winter when he wrote:

A winter such as when birds die
In the deep forests, and the fishes lie
Stiffened in the translucent ice, which makes
Even the mud and slime of the warm lakes
A wrinkled cold as hard as bricks; and when
Among their children, comfortable men
Gather about great fires, and yet feel cold;
Alas! then for the homeless beggar old!

However civilized we may become, the two extremes of fortune remain. And in these days of war the beggar is not the only homeless individual, and many have lost their homes without the agency of winter and snow.

An ancient Chinese story relates that about the sixth century BC there was for three days a heavy fall of snow in Chi State. The ruler, Duke Ching, clad in a white fox-fur coat, remarked in surprise to his minister Yen Tzu that he had not felt cold. "The Sage ruler of old," answered Yen Tzu, "visualized others hungry when *he* was not hungry, and realized that others might be cold even when he himself was warm." The Duke understood the rebuke, took off his fur coat for his minister to sell, and ordered from the State barn a large quantity of rice to be distributed among the cold and hungry. He was indeed a good and honest man. But what of those who now gather about fires and yet feel cold? Might they not grumble about the strict rationing of coal in wartime, even if there were another Yen Tzu to remind them of their cold and hungry fellows? Might they not forget that many of their compatriots are away fighting in biting winds and snow-bound battlefields?

Duke Ching was fortunate to be in a position to discard his fur coat and distribute rice; I am differently placed. What was *I* to do when I heard the hungry chirp of a tiny bird on the bush outside my window? Snow must have fallen heavily in the night, for it was a foot deep, and my eyes were dazzled by its glittering whiteness. I hurried downstairs, resolved to share a little of my breakfast bread with the birds. But the one which had chirped outside my window had already flown away, having perhaps given up all hope of getting food; so, wrapping up the crumbs in a paper bag, and putting on my overcoat, I went out for a walk in the snow.

The milkboy had just finished his round. The horse's footprints and the tracks of the cart stood out clearly. Many people were sweeping their doorsteps, with rhythmical sounds and movements. My head was refreshed by the cold air and I composed a little poem:

一夜飛花白古城行來
不覺此身輕玉塵鋪
地頻回首且聽家家
掃雪聲
牛津雪霽 啞

A night of flying petals has whitened the old city,
I walk along not realizing the lightness of my
body.
Jade dust paves the road; I turn my head from
time to time.
Listen, listen to the sound of snow being swept
away from door to door.

I came to Kingston Road, where a great roaring and shouting greeted me. A snow fight was in progress, the boys being divided into two groups. Some had got hold of dustbin lids and were using them as shields like warriors of old. It was a comical sight.

Though walking slowly, my feet trod lightly on the snow, and it did not take me long to get to Port Meadow by way of Aristotle Lane. There I stopped to admire some rugged willows of great beauty, whose myriad slender branches and elegant twigs intermingled in intricate patterns. Suddenly a small shower of white powder fell, or rather was shaken, from one of the lower thicker branches. I looked up in surprise, for there was at that moment neither wind nor snowfall. It was a redbreast, that daring and sociable creature, hopping from branch to branch and chirping as if for food. I remembered my errand, and threw some

Snowball fight

breadcrumbs. Birds are usually shy creatures; they do not really like man's company, nor do they trust him; and as I am not a very sociable person myself I try not to interfere with them. But the redbreast is an exception; he seems to have faith in man, and seldom forgets to bring himself to my notice whenever possible.

My redbreast ventured down and pecked at the crumbs, stopped for another peck, then flew up to his branch again, his keen little eyes fixed on me and begging for some more. He was indeed an open-hearted creature. Meanwhile two or three sparrows cautiously yet cheekily hopped along behind him, and I had to throw more crumbs. A blackbird, saucy fellow, was quick to see them, and swooped to peck one of the biggest crumbs, which served only to whet his appetite, the glutton! Then came another blackbird, a third, a fourth, a fifth. I threw all the crumbs I had and stepped away a little distance in order to see the charming picture of willows and the black forms of birds against the white shroud of snow.

More birds, including many blackbirds, arrived with extraordinary speed. The paper bag was soon empty, and I felt that my mission was at an end. I left the birds gobbling the remnants of their feast.

Standing at the edge of the Meadow, I looked at the vast flat stretch of whiteness whose cold purity brought peace to the heart. So much snow had fallen that the low meadow had been raised to the level of the footpath, which is slightly higher. It seemed that the earth had been lifted closer to the sky, its surface broadened, and distant objects brought into clearer view. I could distinctly see the little village of Binsey, and Wytham Hill too, usually hidden by tall trees on the river-bank behind. Yet everything was in miniature: the trees, the village houses, and Wytham Hill, though sharp in outline, resembled a miniature bas-relief, as did the village of Wolvercote.

A man and a dog were coming towards me, apparently without legs, for the stillness and the soft atmosphere, with the low-hanging grey sky, seemed to deny all movement.

From my left, nearby, came the clamour of skaters, and I watched them for a while. Far beyond I saw the slender tower of St. Barnabas, piercing the sky. Then by way of Willow Walk I reached the snow-laden wooden bridge. The Thames was not frozen and the water flowed steadily, dark against the snowy banks, where in warm weather it had gleamed against the darker grass. What infinite variety the seasons give!

I was surprised to see a fisherman sitting in the snow at the far end of another wooden bridge, and I thought of a famous T'ang poem by Liu Tsung-yuan:

Not a bird among the thousand mountains;
Not a footprint on the myriad footpaths.
In a lonely boat an old fisherman with bamboo-hat and grass-coat
Is fishing in the cold snowy river.

I thought also of that masterpiece, "A Fisherman in Snow", by an unknown artist of the Five Dynasties (AD 907-959), which was shown at the Chinese Art Exhibition at Burlington House in 1935-6. When eventually I reached his haunt I saw that he was well protected by a thick yellow mackintosh and high wellington boots, and was smoking a pipe. He turned and smiled at me, and I smiled back. No word was spoken. There were no "thousand mountains" around us, and no snow-laden bamboo was to be seen; but the English fisherman, Wytham Hill, and the long reeds by the river, made a perfect picture all the same.

On the footpath, with water running almost, parallel on both sides, I met no one. If I ignored the existence of the modern waterworks in the distance, it was not unlike my accustomed haunts in China. One of the T'ang poets, Meng Hao-yuan, often used to ride in the snow on a donkey in search of winter-plum blossom, and this was considered a highly romantic and poetic thing to do. Another poet, Yuan Teh-ming, of the Sung Dynasty, once described his own walk in the snow in two lines:

I myself am in the scene and can have no words to describe it,
But I would like to let others compare Meng and me.

I felt rather the same way.

Presently I crossed the main road to Old Osney, still following the river-bank. The people living in the houses facing the river apparently did not trouble about the snow on their doorsteps. By the waterworks I beheld a perfect silhouette of Oxford against a white background:

Tom Tower and St. Mary's spire, packed with many others in a black mass in the distance, deep snow covering the roofs around. The city seemed small enough to pick up in my hand. I felt like Gulliver in Lilliput.

When I reached Folly Bridge it began to snow again, and not wishing to wander too far I turned into Christ Church Meadow. The snow-flakes first danced merrily in minute particles, then fell more steadily in larger flakes until they seemed to colour the air around me and I could no longer see the meadow. I was reminded of a visit I had once paid to Kew Gardens in late spring. I had been standing under a huge pear-tree in full bloom, and thousands of soft white petals had fallen around me.

On the banks of the Cherwell I could hear the soft, pleasant sound of snow falling on the withered reeds. A charming old Chinese couplet describes it better than I can:

Striking on the windows it sounds like silkworms nibbling mulberry leaves;
Falling on the bamboos it suggests crabs crawling on the sand.

When at last I found myself in the High I felt I had walked a long way, for my legs refused to move more quickly. From the entrance to Queen's College I had an uninterrupted view of the High, which was practically clear of traffic and seemed wider on account of the unswept snow. Every footprint and car-track was revealed, and the wheel-marks had formed an intricate pattern.

I have often wondered why Oxford 'buses are painted scarlet, for the colour does not go well with the yellow-grey of the buildings, but when I saw a 'bus halted by St. Mary's Church and noticed the vivid splash of colour against the white snow, I thought I knew the reason: though doubtless the 'bus company had not chosen this particular colour with any aesthetic effect in mind!

They say it does not often snow in Oxford in winter. Perhaps I have been lucky.

A youth, with the long sleeves of his black college gown flying behind him, came riding a bicycle down the middle of the street, and I reflected that no matter how things change, Oxford still belongs to the undergraduates.

In China our professional artists or craftsmen used to carve large pieces of white ivory into models of famous buildings, such as the Peking Palace or the Temple of Heaven, with streets and people to the minutest detail. I have been fortunate enough to see a few of these, and the snow-covered Oxford High, with its yellow stone, resembled one of these exquisite ivory carvings, yellowed with age. I was happy to have discovered such affinity between Oxford and Ancient China.

A Snowy Night in Oxford

At midnight the cold creeps in and I drink tea instead of wine;
Oh, the gentle sound on the small window of snow blown by the wind!
In Oxford I have twice seen winter's arrival and departure:
Who can have the same deep longing as I have now for my homeland?

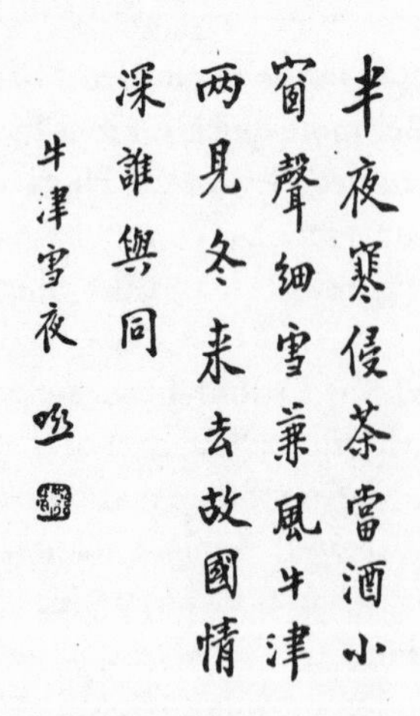

6
The Three Little Cherry-Trees

WHENEVER I go by Broad Walk in Christ Church Meadow I stop to admire the three little cherry-trees standing negligently in the left corner by the wall of Meadow Building. I doubt if I should ever have noticed them had I not once seen them in bloom.

It was on a misty morning in April 1941. I was new to Oxford then, but I had already made a habit of taking a morning walk round the meadow, generally entering by the Memorial Gate. Attracted by the tall trees bordering Broad Walk and veiled with many-shaded mists in autumn and winter, I used to turn to the right at the end of the Walk along the River Cherwell, passing the college barges. For some time I did not know of the existence of these three little cherry-trees.

Memorial Gate

Then, one morning, I went a different way—past the car-park instead of by the Memorial Gate. Before reaching the end of the sidewalk I caught sight of the cherry-trees crowned with a mass of pink blossoms and tiny greenish leaves. Their grace and charm and their pretty garments were like the fresh bloom of maidenhood. I went towards them. The yellowish wall of the ancient college building and the distant, tall, impressive trees along Broad Walk seemed to pale and lose their significance. Yet I alone among the many people in the meadow was admiring the cherry-trees, which the drizzling rain of the previous night had brought into their full glory.

The following morning, however, when I went again, many other admirers were there too. But the west wind became restive, and a few mornings later the beautiful blossoms had already begun to fall round the feet of the trees. Soon the gardener had swept away their bedraggled garments, and all trace of their glory was gone. No one came to look at the tracery of their branches, bare save for the green leaves which came out later, and perhaps they have since been forgotten. But *I* cannot forget their short-lived splendour, and I always remember them when I pass, though the magic of that time has vanished, for I can no longer withstand the censure of the college building and of the tall trees. Christ Church upbraids me for having neglected it; the tall trees have risen again to their full stature and have shown their magnanimity in welcoming me as usual, and I feel ashamed of my fickleness.

Robert Herrick once wrote:

Ye may simper, blush and smile,
And perfume the air a-while:
But (sweet things) ye must be gone;
Fruit, ye know, is coming on:
Then, ah! then, where is your grace,
Whenas Cherries come in place?

Alas! These three little cherry-trees were either too small to bear fruit or else they were not the fruit-bearing species. I have seen their grace, but that lasted so short a time, and now they are unnoticed and ignored. Can it be that human sentiment is only roused when the object of its admiration is in its prime? Does affection for it die when its full glory has begun to fade? If so, it would seem as if the love and indifference in mankind depend on outward form rather than on inward feeling, and I must myself be careful not to be misled by a show of affection!

While in blossom the cherry-trees had been proud of their beauty, and the admiration of human beings had seemed to intensify their colour. But when their full glory began to fade, and people no longer came to admire them, they grew more and more depressed. Now they have no more tears to shed and are bereft of human admiration. Did they know that their short-lived glory would be followed by such dismal neglect? Is it possible to control our natural pride in achievement even while realizing the ephemeral nature of things? Perhaps the cherry-trees were not concerned with this problem, for, after all, will they not bloom again next year? But we sensitive human creatures must reflect on these aspects of our lives. William Blake once wrote: "Excess of sorrow laughs. Excess of joy weeps."

I remembered a story in Hua-shih, a Chinese history of flowers, about Chang Mou-ching, who was very fond of beautiful girls. One day he saw a cherry-tree in bloom, so he brought wine to drink in its shade, declaring that the cherry blossoms were even more beautiful than women. In that moment he became aware of the secret of life, and avoided young girls thereafter. It is curious that this old boy should have found the secret of life in this way without realizing his own weakness. Oh! pretty girls, enjoy yourselves while you are still beautiful, but you cannot live on beauty alone!

Another story came into my mind from Kou-nü-chi, a tale of a jealous girl. The daughter of Wu Li-yang was married to Yuan Hsuan, whose behaviour she watched jealously. When the peach-tree in the family garden was in bloom Yuan Hsuan went out to admire it and praised so highly the beauty of its blossoms that his wife cut down the tree with an axe and trampled on the blossoms. She thought that if he behaved like this, he would give his praise to any pretty girl he chanced to meet. What strength her anger gave her! I only hope that those who have already admired these three little cherry-trees in Oxford have not had trouble with their wives or lady-friends. But English girls have practical minds and will not think of cherry blossoms as rivals in the way we Chinese like to compare girls and flowers: so these three little cherry-trees can still stand in the left corner by the wall of Christ Church, without fear of causing matrimonial strife.

7
"I Do Like Thee, River Cherwell"

OXFORD, unlike London, is a different city on Sunday morning. The delightful emptiness of the streets emphasizes the fine architecture of the buildings in the magnificent High Street. On weekdays, especially during the rush hours, the South Porch and beautiful spire of St. Mary-the-Virgin's Church seem insignificant, while the tall rumbling 'buses are most conspicuous; the top of Queen's College Gateway, University College, All Souls', and the Examination School appear in no way superior to many big business premises such as the Westminster Bank. But on Sunday morning, when there are no people and traffic about, the silence and emptiness reveal the true worth of these beautiful edifices.

When I stroll down High Street on Sunday mornings I feel I am seeing the real charm and beauty of Oxford. I seem to grow smaller, for the street is so dignified and spacious in its solitude, and the aloof grandeur of the ancient buildings is revealed.

The long winding stretch leading from Queen's College to Magdalen Bridge is always tempting and attractive, though the bridge cannot actually be seen. I suppose the greyish-yellow walls of Magdalen are more or less the same colour as those of Queen's or All Souls' but they certainly look brighter; for Magdalen stands at the end of "the High", framed by the River Cherwell and stretches of bright green meadow.

I do not know why High Street is so empty on Sunday mornings; nor why the 'buses should not run before twelve o'clock. This suspension of 'buses on Sunday mornings, which was, I believe, started before the war, empties the streets conveniently for a morning stroll. Oxford is, after all, an inland city of learning, not essentially a commercial or industrial centre.

One Sunday, on a cold sunny early April morning, I walked leisurely along High Street to Longwall Street. There were a few uniformed people about, and my eyes fell suddenly on a group of choir-boys in black and white gowns and square caps crossing the street to Magdalen College. Then came five adults in distinguished gowns with ceremonial staffs in their hands, one of whom I recognized as the President of Magdalen, Professor Gordon, who has since died. (I had met him once at a literary party in London, but I do not suppose he remembered me.) I wanted to see more of them, but hesitated to walk more quickly as I did not know whether I should be allowed to go to the service; but when I read the notice at the college entrance, "This college is now open to visitors from 10 a.m. to 6 p.m.", I walked in.

The church service was nearly over: but the thing that interested me was the engraved stone figure of a Saint on the left wall near the door, which closely resembled figures on the walls of certain ancient Chinese temples. The sculpture, and the attitude of the Saint, with hands folded, was identical with that of ancient Chinese stone-rubbings and figure-paintings. How close in their conception of art in olden times were the English and the Chinese! And how, in succeeding centuries, have the cultures of these two people deviated, rendered complex and at variance by the practices of ambitious seekers after fame and gold.

Magdalen—staircase to the hall

Leaving the cloister by a passage on the north side of the college, I came to the spacious lawn. The flowers bordering the lawn were not yet in bloom, and the gardeners were busy preparing for the coming show. I crossed the stone bridge outside the Iron Gate. I imagine that the water flowing beneath is a part of the Cherwell—possibly the only part where boats cannot pass. On the opposite side of the Water Walks, facing the stone bridge, was a mass of white, yellow and purple crocuses in their last glory, and I even found a few bedraggled snowdrops. One or two tiny daisy buds were peeping out through their green collars, and groups of narcissi would soon be in bloom. The big wide leaves of the irises caught my eye, and a few tiny wild blue flowers whose name I did not know were dotted here and there. Among the flowers was a notice on a piece of wood: "Do not touch these Flowers".

A ginger cat which I had seen sitting on the grass near the flowers was now lounging on the path basking in the sunshine, and I wondered why it had moved. Was it fond of flowers? Or had it acquired a certain facility for reading notices, having lived in the vicinity of so learned an institution as Magdalen College? I believe the cat belongs to the College cook, for I have often seen it lying in the entrance to the College kitchen. I remembered a quotation from the preface to Bernard Shaw's *Back to Methuselah*:

> *When I was a child and was told that our dog and our parrot, with whom I was on intimate terms, were not creatures like myself, but were brutal whilst I was reasonable, I not only did not believe it, but quite consciously and intellectually formed the opinion that the distinction was false: so that afterwards, when Darwin's views were first unfolded to me I promptly said that I had found out all that for myself before I was ten years old: and I am far from sure that my youthful arrogance was not justified; for this sense of the kinship of all forms of life is all that is needed to make Evolution not only a conceivable theory, but an inspiring one.*

But G. B. S. is, after all, a more direct descendant of Darwin than we Chinese. He is imbued with the theory of Evolution and retains the belief in man's superiority. Our great philosophers believe that man is but one of the million creatures sharing in some degree the mysteries of life and death.

The trees in the deer park were not yet leaf-covered, and the deer, lying in the sun, were clearly visible.

The following passage occurs in Anthony à Wood's *Annals* (1586):

> *Certain scholars of Magdalen College stealing deer in the Forest of Shotover belonging to the King, one of them named Thomas Godstow, of Magdalen College, was taken, carried before the Lord Norreys and by him imprisoned. The rest of his fellows resenting the matter resolve with a party that they would make an assault on him the next time he came to Oxford. The Quarter Sessions drawing near, which were about Michaelmas, the Lord Norreys with his retinew came to Oxford and loged himself in the Bear Inn, near All Saints Church. The said scholars having notice of it, gather together with their gowns girt about them, armed with divers sorts of weapons and coming courageously up to the said Inn, made an assault on some of the Lord's retinew, intending at length to lay hold on the Lord himself. But timely notice being given to him, he sends out his son Maximilian attended with his servants, and making an onset on the scholars, beat them down as far as St. Mary's Church. Whereupon a great outcrie being raised, the Vice-chancellor, Proctors and others are called, who rushing suddenly in among the Scholars appeased and sent them away with fair words, yet some of them were hurt, and Binks the Lord's keeper sorely wounded.*
>
> *Soon after the Vice-chancellor sent word to all Heads of Houses, that they should command their Scholars into their respective Colleges, which being accordingly done and all kept within, the Lord departed the Town. But the Scholars of Magdalen College being not able to pocket these affronts, went up privately to the top of their Tower and waiting till he should pass by towards Ricot sent down a shower of stones that they had picked up, upon him and his retinew, wounding some and endangering others of their lives. It is said that upon the foresight of this storm, divers had got boards, others tables on their heads to keep them from it, and that if the Lord had not been in his coach or chariot he would certainly have been killed.* [1]

Certainly the ancestors of these deer now in the park had nothing to do with the said Scholars of 1586, because the deer park was occupied by Prince Rupert in the Civil War between 1644 and 1646. I was amused to know that English scholars behaved in those days no better than Chinese scholars.

My attention strayed from the deer park, and I followed the sound of running water beneath a house said to have been an old water-mill. The water poured in at this narrow part of the Cherwell, and at this time of the year joined the Thames at Folly Bridge. The gurgle of running water has a soothing and clarifying effect on the mind, particularly when heard amid the rush and bustle of a town. I stood for a while, and then followed two ducks swimming down the river until I came to the delightful avenue known as Addison's Walk. Scholars have often disputed whether Addison ever actually walked there. The point was not important to me. But I asked: Did he write about the Walk, where the kingfisher "flashes down the river, a flame of blue"? He cannot have walked alone, for even I had the ducks and birds to keep me company.

I sat down on the seat at the end of the Walk. On the left there is a wooden bridge which bears a notice: "For the use of members of Magdalen College only", so I did not attempt to cross over. Instead I continued my walk along the riverside, where a flock of small birds—robins and blue-tits—were gaily hopping about the road and jumping from branch to branch of the shrubs and trees. The robins seemed to seek the limelight, either perching on a bare branch or on the fence, in full view of the world. I thought once as I walked on that the same robin had followed me along, but later saw one or two more.

I was now standing beside a small pond inside the College field. At the edge, the long slender branches of two young weeping willows drooped gracefully down to the water. Two ducks were happily diving, and washing their backs with great energy. I wonder if they were the same two whose acquaintance I had made a short while before?

On the river to my left a boat approached with two undergraduates on board. One was rowing; the other, book in hand, was reading aloud—perhaps a poem—as if to himself, although his companion was listening intently.

From the big gap in the trees where I stood I now had a clear view of the whole college field, and of the three tall weeping willows by Addison's Walk. On their slender branches were the young tiny leaves, whose loose

Tom Tower in mist

Lapwings over Merton Field

silky robes were reflected golden-yellow in the sun. Lying expressionless and contented in the field were six black cows, whose appearance in the college grounds reminded the unappreciative that even so erudite an institution as this had a rural setting. In China we see cows only in the country, and many a compatriot of mine, travelling from town to town and seeing cows in all the fields, might well mistake England for a predominantly agricultural country. The cows in Oxford, however, are not as friendly as those in the Yorkshire Dales, perhaps because they are so accustomed to human beings and are not impressed by them. The six black cows in the college field did not even look my way!

On the left, through the still bare trees, Magdalen Tower stood in perfect silhouette, blue-black against the sun.

With the exception of the two undergraduates in the boat I met nobody until I reached the end of the Water Walks, when I met two more undergraduates walking in my direction. Each carried a stick and one, wearing a new fashionable brown suit with very broad shoulders, smoked a pipe in expert manner, while the other, smoking a cigarette, walked with his head high in the air. They were so deep in conversation that they did not even look at each other as they talked. I watched them with interest until they were out of sight.

Two undergraduates walking

Eventually I came to a side-door of the college—perhaps a back-door of the College kitchen—where there was a bicycle stand, and an enormous accumulation of wine and beer bottles in an orderly row along the wall. I doubt if the inspectors of the Ministry of Food will make trouble with the college authorities, for these bottles looked quite antique and were probably kept there to enhance the antiquity of the college.

I crossed the road and walked along the river-bank round the Botanic Garden, passing through the gate from Rose Lane to Broad Walk, Christ Church. From here the Cathedral and the Hall of Christ Church are quite clearly visible, with Tom Tower, a little farther distant, between them. I skirted the long avenue and walked beside the river, of which I never weary, for the scenery is so varied. The trees here are beautiful, and in early spring, while the leaves are still in bud, they are fascinating to observe. The river was still, and the trees reflected in its calm depths were lovelier than ever. The tips of their intertwining branches, obscure in outline, seemed to mingle with the reflected clouds and blue-grey sky. Nothing stirred; nothing vibrated; the river had almost ceased to run; and the stillness produced a cathartic effect on me, cleansing my mind of many foolish thoughts and unnecessary worries.

I sat down by a ferry, where there used at one time to be a square barge towed by a piece of thick rope. This time neither the boat nor the thick cord was to be seen. I have never yet crossed to the other side, though the long footpath leading to some unknown destination looked interesting and inviting. In a pleasantly relaxed state of mind, I looked around. A noise in the grass caught my attention, but for a while I could see nothing that could have caused it. Then suddenly a fat toad or greenish-grey frog leapt out of the grass into the middle of the footpath. It paused for a moment, its huge eyes seeming to look sideways at me, its fleshy throat moving incessantly. Was it panting, tired by its struggle to get clear of the grass? I made no sound; all was quiet, and the little animal was content to stay for a short while. Then it continued to leap until it plunged into the water. A small whirling wrinkle appeared on the surface and vanished almost at once, and there was no further sign of the toad's activities.

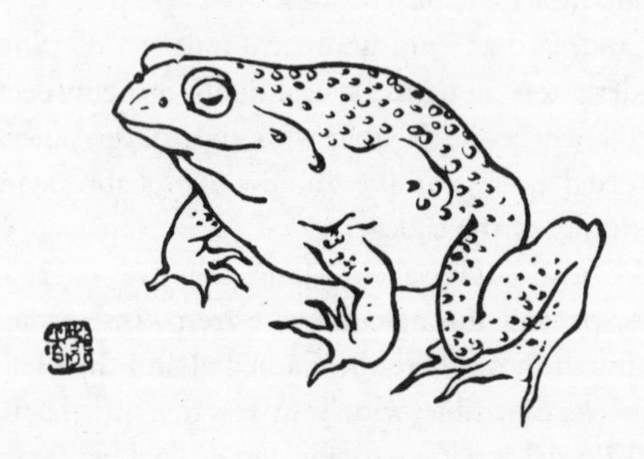

A little rest?

I had seen the deluge of water pouring into the river through the old water-mill by the Water Walks of Magdalen College, and had noticed a number of fish near Magdalen Bridge, and I thought how true and right Lao-tzu had been when he said: "The highest good is like that of water. The goodness of water is that it benefits the ten thousand creatures, yet itself does not grumble." [2] Again, he remarked: "As the heavy must be the foundation of the light, so quietness is lord and master of activity." [3] I was engulfed in a great quietness, yet one in which everything was invisibly active and alive. Only, quietness without activity means death or stagnation; and in early spring the quiet womb of earth is astir with young pulsating life.

Lifting my head to breathe deeply of the sweet air, I caught sight of a small bird perched on a low branch stretching out to the middle of the river, perfectly reflected in the water. It too had perhaps been watching the antics of the toad, and kept turning its head round in an effort to see how it had disappeared. A big black spot on the top of the bird's head interested me, for I thought it might be a blackcap about which I had been reading in books on British birds. I was glad to have seen it, but I wished I could have heard it singing, for the beauty of its song is said to be second only to that of the nightingale. It did chirp a few notes, however, and I noticed that as it produced the sounds its "black cap" seemed to rise. It reminded me of brown Capuchin monkeys which also have a "black cap" on top of their heads. How akin are many varied forms of life in Nature!

A blackcap

A young couple in Air Force uniform—the first human beings I had seen on that part of the river—strolling along the path, had sent the blackcap away. Their heads were close together, and their arms were clasped round each other's waist. They walked very slowly, talking happily in low voices and showing no embarrassment in spite of their

Walking along the Cherwell

uniform. Uniform or no uniform, life must go on I thought of all the couples in civilian clothes: couples walking here before the first world war; in Elizabethan costume; in Georgian costume; in Victorian costume. Though through successive generations men may differ outwardly, yet fundamentally they do not change. They may talk in the language of Chaucer, of Bacon, of Shakespeare, or of Churchill; but the essence of life remains as it has always been. Those who would change the world succeed in changing *only* its surface: the core remains inviolate. The world of nature, direct and simple in its needs, never changes; trees, grass, flowers, birds, frogs, water, do not seek variation in their existence: man is the only complex creature.

I was becoming involved again, so I moved on. A punt came gliding down the river, expertly manoeuvred by a young undergraduate. He wielded the long pole slowly and gracefully, and the boat moved smoothly, scarcely disturbing the water. Since I came to Oxford I have found great pleasure in watching the punts making their leisurely way up and down the river, and have spent many hours watching them from the banks of the river in University Park. I sometimes wonder what the undergraduates would do besides punting during their summer terms, for they are nearly always to be seen on the river in the afternoons. The more experienced of them were so attractive to watch that I made several little sketches of them. Once or twice I have tried to punt myself, but my hands were clumsy, the pole would not obey, and I discovered that I was apparently a source of annoyance to other punters, who kept frowning to me.

Female punters

The punt glided out of sight, and I strolled on until I came to a timber bridge leading to a boat-house. If the bridge had not been painted white, and if the college barge had been absent, the background of waterways and the tall trees would have been almost identical with certain parts of central China.

As I went homewards through the Memorial Gate I thought that this had been one of the most pleasant mornings I had spent by the Cherwell. I could only express myself adequately by changing one or two words from the well-known verses about Dr. Fell:

I do like thee, River Cherwell,
The reason why I cannot tell.
But only this I know full well,
I do like thee, River Cherwell.

[1] Quoted from Lewis and Fenby's *Anatomy of Oxford* (Jonathan Cape).

[2] and [3] Both quoted from Arthur Waley's excellent book, *The Way and Its Power* (George Allen and Unwin).

Male punters

8
The Wine of Heaven

MANY of our great poets have described rain as tears shed by heaven in sympathy for long-suffering humanity, and most of our best thinkers have thought of it as a life-giving liquid animating all creatures. But *I* like to call it the wine of heaven, for though I am no drinker and my face always turns red when I have had a little wine, my spirits rise. Like me, flowers take on a fresher colour in the drizzling rain; the leaves look greener, the tree-trunks darker; and the feathers of birds are smoother and glossier. Rain washes the dust from buildings; it stirs the surface of lakes and rivers; it erects a natural screen that is a great beautifier of ordinary everyday things.

But rain may prevent pretty girls from going out in their new hats and fashionable frocks. Rain makes the faces of college professors frown and shrink. It cannot be very attractive to undergraduates who cannot change their trousers often or brush their shoes; nor to housewives, factory-workers and business men who have to tramp through the mud.

For myself, in spite of the inconvenience to my feet and the trouble of drying my soaked clothes, I like strolling in the rain, and in Oxford rain is as plentiful as in most other parts of England.

Here are five little stories about rain.

One afternoon I was exploring St. John's College garden. At one corner of the rockery was a small healthy tree-lupin in its fresh green coat. The leaves of the lupin, evenly arranged six or eight to each spray, have always seemed to me a perfect pattern for decorative design. A tiny drop of rain, like a transparent crystal or pearl reflecting the light, was concealed at the base of each spray where the ends of the leaves meet, additional ornaments in a beautiful pattern. I tried to imagine the glistering drops surrounded by lupin leaves on a pretty girl's dance frock, and thought how charming it would look.

First quad, St. John's College

On another occasion I was strolling in the grounds in front of the new buildings of Magdalen College, looking at the bright flower-beds surrounding the spacious lawn. The flowers were opening wide their tiny mouths to drink the rain. "You should not drink so much", I wanted to warn them, "for it will spoil your looks." The rain was heavier than usual, a thick screen of glassy needles all around me. I leaned on the railings of the deer park for a while. Three or four deer, nibbling the grass under the huge leafy trees, seemed unaware of the rain. I could not see the fine silver lines against the dark depths of the trees, but I liked listening to the pattering on the leaves, which unfortunately drowned the sound of the deer nibbling. As I moved slowly back from the railings the glassy screen was drawn in front of me again. I noticed with some surprise that the thin needles seemed joined to the tiny white spots on the backs of some of the deer, though sometimes the connexion was practically invisible. Suddenly the white spots seemed to shoot up like searchlights to the sky, making me think of a theatre stage with the trees as background and the deer as puppets. I preferred to have the trouble of drying my wet clothes to missing this unique experience.

One summer afternoon I was going fishing with the Keene family along the lower part of the Cherwell when it began to rain. Actually only Mr. Keene fished; his family and I were mere spectators. I strolled off for a while to explore the countryside. When I came back Mr. Keene told me that he had caught two or three small roach or perch, but had thrown them back into the water. When the rain became really heavy, we set off for home. We had to walk a long way through Marston Ferry Road to Banbury Road. Mr. Keene, fishing rods and sack on his back, strode along with Terry, his nephew, who had been evacuated from London. Mrs. Keene held her daughter Rita's hand, and I walked a little distance behind them. Both the children had their parents' mackintoshes over their heads so that they were well protected from the rain. The parents urged them to hurry, and the children thought it a grand game and enjoyed themselves immensely.

A gentle wind blew the rain slantwise, like a mass of shiny strings attached to kites high up in the sky. I felt I would like to be holding the strings. I could still hear the pleasant voices of my companions as they hurried through the rain among a crowd of other people also hurrying homewards. It was a happy flight, not a desperate struggle against a storm as I have seen in many seascape paintings. It would be a difficult picture to paint, I thought, as the delicacy of the drizzling light-hearted rain could hardly be so clearly revealed that the picture would not be misinterpreted as a scene in a storm, or a flight sentimentally conceived. But I had forgotten that the surroundings would help to interpret the scene—lovely wet hedges dotted with tiny yellow flowers on both sides of the path, and tree-tops blown in the same direction as the slant of the rain. If their grace and their shiny wetness could be perfectly painted, and the fine drizzle of rain executed sensitively, a sort of happy sympathy for the runaways would be automatic. That, however, would depend on how large a place in the picture the figures would take. I walked more slowly, letting my friends recede from me until they ceased to occupy a dominant position in the landscape, yet remained necessary and important factors. It seemed to me an extraordinarily beautiful picture. My thanks are due to the Wine of Heaven for teaching me a new approach to my painting.

I was intoxicated yet another time by this heady wine. One evening I was watching the rain over the meadow which stretches from Magdalen Bridge along the side of Magdalen College. On the Botanic Garden side I was at once attracted by the reflections of the whirling bicycle-wheels on the wet bridge and did not want to look farther, so I sat down on a nearby seat. Many factory-workers and shop-assistants were bicycling home at that hour; they were interesting to watch when there were so few cars about. All the wheels rolling along together, with their reflections close beside them, produced a new pattern.

It always annoys me to wait in a queue for a ’bus when it is pouring with rain. Queueing usually means a long wait, and I generally prefer to walk. One familiar and characteristic Oxford scene will always remain in my memory: the approach to St. Michael’s Church from Carfax through Cornmarket Street in rain. In the distance, near the Martyrs’ Memorial, I can see a large crowd under their umbrellas waiting for a Number 2 or a Number 4 ’bus. Before the ’bus draws near to the stop, the crowd, still with umbrellas open, surges forward and forms a large bend in the centre of the road, while the huge bulk of the ’bus rumbles towards the pavement. One morning I said to myself: “There are my umbrellas!” and made a painting of the scene.

It has not been easy to buy barley wine in wartime Oxford. Nevertheless, there will always be the Wine of Heaven for me!

9
A Bit of Temper

ONE chilly, sunny day in mid-April (1941) I felt a great urge to go out. I had no idea where or how far, so to be on the safe side I took sandwiches. In spite of the sun there was a heavy morning mist. St. Barnabas Tower was in faint outline, and I could not see far beyond the boathouse with its strings of boats for hire. This in no way damped my spirits, and I felt very cheerful strolling along and thinking of nothing in particular. Longfellow's translation of "The Terrestrial Paradise" reflected my mood:

> *Without more delay I left the bank,*
> *Crossing the level country slowly, slowly,*
> *Over the soil, that everywhere breathed fragrance.*
>
> *A gently-breathing air, that no mutation*
> *Had in itself, smote me upon the forehead,*
> *No heavier blow, than of a pleasant breeze.*

I was seeing another English spring, whose first breath had already reached Oxford.

From the big wooden bridge over the Thames I tried to pick out well-known landmarks. A fisherman nearby was visible, but the bridge on which he stood was cloaked in mist, and he appeared to be sitting on air. I was reminded of a painting by the renowned monk-artist Shih Tao, of the Late Ming Dynasty (about the beginning of the seventeenth century), which depicts a fisherman sitting on a small bridge fishing, the man far bigger than the bridge and his gown nearly covering it. The few trees and the distant hills are beautifully composed and the brushwork perfectly executed. At the first glance the bridge appears hardly capable of supporting the man, but this impression disappears on closer inspection. Now I realized the reason. Shih Tao was famous for his brushwork, which made full use of the subtle tones of the ink, and also for his composition, which seldom followed but rather improved on the traditions of T'ang and Sung. He has become the undisputed great master of the last three hundred years. Many Western connoisseurs have paid little attention to Chinese art produced after the Sung and Yüan periods, they have undervalued the later period because they have not understood the possibilities of our brushes and inks. Had the French Impressionists been able to see some of Shih Tao's original works, they might have cultivated their "modern" style with less labour. The creation of a great work of art requires more than the precise rendering of perspective and meticulous realism: it demands poetic exaggeration of the impression made on the artist's sensitive mind. Shih Tao was right to exaggerate the size of his fisherman, and here I should like to thank my distant fisherman for opening my eyes to the truth.

A sudden whim made me hire a boat. But not for the purpose of physical exercise: a blistered palm will never be mine; nor would I dream of purposefully tiring my body. But here was just the opportunity to get myself afloat, for there was not a single other boat to be seen on the river, and there was therefore no danger of my proving myself a nuisance to fellow-boaters. I pulled in the direction of Godstow, alternately rowing a little and then letting the boat drift. Time existed no more; the river was mine. After a few pulls (I have lost the habit of rowing in the Chinese manner by *pushing*) I felt warm. The morning mist had dispersed, though the village of Godstow was still not very clear. I drifted along, rowing leisurely, the meadow seeming to rise high above the river, the long reeds near the shore towering above me. I crept along behind the reeds, not wishing to disturb a flock of geese a little way ahead of me. Fascinated, I watched the reeds brushed by the gentle wind in one direction; then, as they righted themselves, they seemed to tease the wind, throwing back their heads until they were gathered up once more and brushed forward.

I drifted on. Looking up at the bank opposite the meadow, I remembered a simple poem by Mei Yao-cheng of Sung dynasty, and recited it aloud in my own language:

On the banks are the dense grass and thick woods.
I do not often know what they are called.
There are singing birds there,
Which seem to be welcoming my boat.

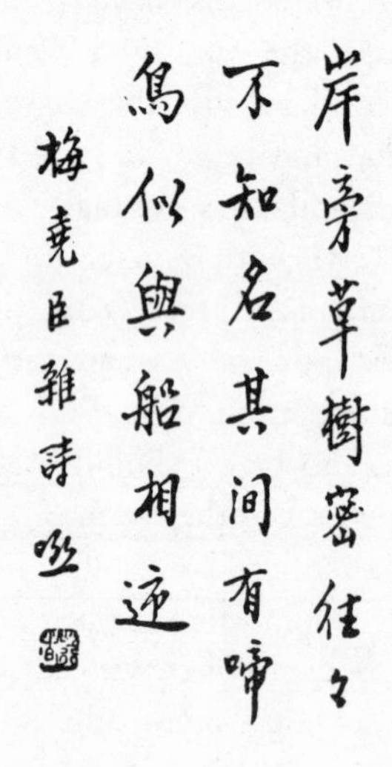

As I neared the sign-post bearing the word "Perch" I remembered also a poem by my favourite poet Li P'o of T'ang dynasty:

For love of this gentle stream,
I ride on the wavelets with endless joy.
Moving the oars only slightly not to startle the sea-gulls,
I throw my line and wait for the fish to bite.
The waves tease the reflection of the morning clouds.
On the banks are piled up the colours of spring hills.
Where has the "washing silk" lady come from—
A ruddy young face that I do not know?

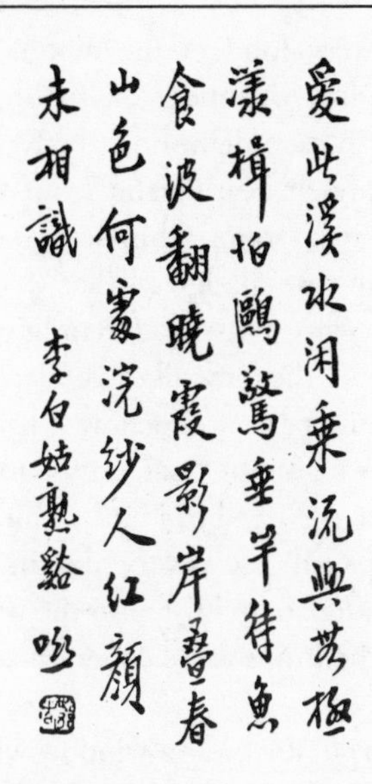

There was, strangely enough, someone in a red overall leaning over the water just in front of the sign-post; it was the first person I had seen. I certainly had no idea who she was.

London sea-gulls do not as a rule frequent this part of the Thames, but I could hear the intermittent cry of lapwings flying above Port Meadow. Their cry is not unlike the cry of sea-gulls, but a little too melancholy: I now prefer the fiercer note of gulls, perhaps because I became used to it in London. I have always said that should I have to leave this country there are three things I should deeply miss: the green grass of London parks, the sea-gulls over the London river, and the pigeons in the squares. The grass in Oxford is still as green as ever, but I often miss the sea-gulls and pigeons.

Once rowing on the Thames near Richmond Park I composed a little poem:

With a book of Li P'o's poems,
I sit in a melon-shaped boat drifting in the wind
With no hat on my head and my face turned to the sky I recite aloud,
And wonder to whom the moonlight belongs tonight?

Like Li P'o I am very fond of the moon. I have never had the opportunity in England to row under the moon, but how many happy moments have I spent in moonlight on Lake Kang-tang at Kiu-kiang!

Presently I found myself nearing the Trout Inn. I was already well acquainted with this inn; some Chinese friends of mine had first introduced me to it, and we all agreed that were it not for the stone-carved lion with a crown on its head standing conspicuously in the garden, that garden and the bow-like wooden bridge over the river might almost have been a part of Soochow. I had visited the Trout Inn many a time, but never before by boat. I thought I might as well make a halt there, so I tied up my boat and climbed out. The inn had apparently just been opened. It was very pleasant to stroll in the garden in the clear April morning air and listen to the water running under the bridge. The owner of the inn is to be congratulated on his efficiency in wartime.

I was seated at a small table near a window when a peacock, with an enchanting tuft on his head, approached me with the slow, stately gait of a prince. He inclined his head to one side and the other and then, by the bridge, turned gracefully round to let the sun shine on his train, which, though not yet very long, dazzled the eye with its rich and varied colours. The backward tilt of his head on his long neck gave his mien a hauteur. He did not glance at me; he saw nobody but himself. I, in my drab and casual clothing, felt very low class, yet sad, also, that this creature should be so snobbish simply on the strength of his handsome plumage.

I opened my packet of sandwiches and scattered some crumbs in the hope of making friends with him. At first he ignored them; then he pecked disinterestedly, and in the end swallowed a few morsels rather condescendingly. I am told that in Italy the peacock is said to have the plumage of an angel, the voice of a devil, and the "guts" of a thief. In China the peacock has always been highly esteemed for its dazzling plumage and elegant carriage, and we use it as decoration in our gardens; sometimes, too, one or two feathers from a peacock's train are put into a rare Sung vase for the study or guest-hall. The peacock has been a favourite subject for our artists for centuries. But I do not remember any reference in Chinese books to its voice or "guts"! I have often heard people in this country say that they loathed the peacock's cry, and considered it unlucky to have a peacock's feather or a picture of a peacock in a room. How different our ideas are! I think nothing in nature can really be said to be perfect, and that is why the peacock has beautiful plumage and a harsh voice. Personally, I don't feel able to pass judgment on the peacock's cry, for I have seldom heard it.

The peacock of the Trout Inn must have been displaying himself to win the attention of two peahens who presently flew down from the roof of the inn to peck some crumbs. Then two girls in brightly coloured dresses came out of the inn, holding glasses of beer, and sat down by the river. They did not notice the peacock, but he noticed them and seemed disturbed by the spectacle. He took a few quick steps, dashed through a fence and disappeared from view. *A bit of temper!* The old Chinese book *Pei-Ya* must be right when it says: "The peacock has a jealous nature. He is very proud of his train. Though he may have been a domestic bird for years, he chases and pecks people in brightly coloured dresses."

An interesting account of the peacock in Buffon's *Natural History* is worth quoting:

> *The Peacock has in some countries been esteemed as an article of luxury; but whatever there may be of delicacy in the flesh of a young Peacock, it is certain an old one is very indifferent eating. Its fame for delicacy, however, did not continue very long; for we find in the time of Francis the First, that it was a custom to serve up Peacocks to the tables of the great, with an intention not to be eaten, but only to be seen. Their manner was to strip off the skin; and then preparing the body with the warmest spices, they covered it up again in its former skin, with all its plumage in full display, and no way injured by the preparation. The bird, thus prepared, was often preserved for many years without corrupting; and it is asserted of the Peacock's flesh, that it keeps longer unputrefied than that of any other animal. To give a higher zest to these entertainments, on weddings particularly, they filled the bird's beak and throat with cotton and camphire, which they set on fire to amuse and delight the company. Peacocks were highly esteemed by the Romans, and the Bible mentions them among Solomon's importations from the East. In the days of chivalry also they were in such great repute as to be the subject of a knightly oath.*

Why have these picturesque customs disappeared?

I waited a while in the hope that the peacock would reappear, but in vain. The happy gossiping of the two girls reminded me that I had had nothing to drink, so I went inside to order a small glass of sherry. At first no one appeared to be serving, though through a doorway I could see a lady busy writing. She paid no attention to me and I felt afraid to disturb her, so I withdrew and sat down outside again at the same table. After a time I re-entered. The lady was still writing, but I bolstered up my courage with the thought: "After all, those girls got something to drink, so why shouldn't I?" And I timidly made my request. "Can't you see", she said, "I am busy finishing a letter?" However, she served me and I thanked her, with apologies. *Another bit of temper!* I thought as I went out to the garden again. But I was not in the least perturbed by what had happened. The pleasant sound of running water reminded me that everything passes away, leaving no trace.

After sipping my sherry I set off to the boat. I walked slowly and stopped to look at the ruins of the old Nunnery, of which I had read the following account in Ward's Oxford Guide book:

> *At Wytham, a path to the right leads to Godstow, where Fair Rosamond spent her last years in religious seclusion. Only the ruins of the Nunnery remain, and, in the matter of romance, Godstow and Woodstock rival Cumnor as disappointments. Furious queens, dagger, and bowl have all been crushed out of spurious existence by hard fact. The truth is sufficiently interesting. King Henry, in remembrance of Rosamond, was a liberal patron of the Nunnery, that is, he made offerings to God out of affection for his mistress. When she died the nuns made a shrine of her tomb. This came to the ears of St. Hugh of Grenoble, Bishop of Lincoln, one of the sweetest characters that ever graced human form, yet absolutely intolerant of sham and cant. He had the remains removed to the cemetery, observing to the nuns that religion made no distinction between the mistress of a King and the mistress of any other man.*

How right he surely was, yet to my mind the Bishop must have been in *a bit of temper* when he spoke those words!

On the return voyage I had a different view of the river. Before I reached the "Perch" sign-post I saw two or three cyclists speeding along the path and shouting loudly. Then in front of my boat appeared a long

The High in snow

Three little cherry-trees

narrow boat containing several white-shirted men, rowing energetically, their bodies swinging backwards and forwards with superb rhythm. Their boat seemed to fly while mine stood still. The cyclists kept abreast of the boat with great enthusiasm. All the boys looked young. What appeared to be the youngest sat in the bow and shouted even more loudly than the cyclists on the bank. He shouted with such vigour, in fact, that I could see nothing of his face but a wide-open mouth which seemed to swallow up his eyes. I was reminded of a *Punch* picture of a street pedlar crying his wares, and an old man bending to speak to him. The caption read: "*Benevolent gentleman*: 'You must be careful, my man, or you will get clergyman's sore throat.'" I should have liked to repeat

Shouting

this to the young man. The noise he made, added to the yells of the cyclists on the footpath, made the river and meadow ring with sound. The noise died away after they had passed, and soon all was quiet and tranquil again. Presently I caught another sound, this time the gentle vibration of the church bell from the church of St. Philip and St. James striking the hour. I did not trouble to count the time; it was enchanting just to listen absently to the chimes winging over the rolling countryside. They do not stir the air like human sounds; they seem feeble in comparison; but in some curious way they emphasize the peace of Nature.

On my way home I indulged in speculation on the subject of rowing. Despite the war, Oxford undergraduates must row. No matter whether they are to be called up in a few days, or in a few months, they must if possible win a Blue before they win the war.

> *Of all the pursuits [wrote J. S. G. Pemberton] to which Oxford undergraduates devote their energies there is none so engrossing as Rowing. Few are the men who despise or affect to despise the rowing element in a College, and in most Colleges a majority of its members have been at one time or other more or less connected with their college boats. This is partly owing to tradition and partly to the commonsense view that rowing is compatible with and ancillary to more serious pursuits.*

During my few years' sojourn in England I have seen many an Englishman, especially if bald-headed and with white moustaches, who, even if in a sour temper or depressed mood, would raise one corner of his mouth in a whimsical smile when the subject of the rowing of his old college cropped up.

There was, however, one man connected with Oxford who did not approve of rowing: John Ruskin, who used to deplore the labour wasted on such unproductive amusement, and tried to substitute for it the useful exercise of road-making! It is said that he once directed a number of undergraduates to repair a road at Hinksey, himself taking a turn with pickaxe and spade. But it was not a success, for even after this effort the road was no better. I know about Ruskin chiefly by his argument with Whistler. Though no one can deny his fineness of character, he seems to me a man always in a temper; for did not his introduction of the uninspiring pastime of road-making clearly betray a *bit of temper?*

10
Harmonious Madness

Teach me half the gladness
That thy brain must know,
Such harmonious madness
From my lips would flow,
The world should listen then, as I am listening now!

To a Skylark: P. B. SHELLEY

IT was not to the harmonious madness from Shelley's lips I had been listening, but to a clamorous chorus of birds' songs, including that of the skylark, on Youlbury Ground. Youlbury Ground is situated on Boar's Hill, which, though very near Oxford, is not actually within its boundaries. No one who visits Oxford fails to visit Boar's Hill, and as I should like to think that they explored Youlbury Ground too, I am including this little article in my book.

I should not have become acquainted with Boar's Hill as soon as a week or two after my arrival in Oxford had I not had an unexpected meeting with Lady Dorothea Hosie, author of *Two Gentlemen of China* and other books.

Not long afterwards I had tea with Lady Hosie at the house of Mrs. Ann Daniels, Elcot Lodge, Boar's Hill. After tea Mrs. Daniels took us for a walk to a small lake somewhere on Boar's Hill, but I did not know then that it was in Youlbury Ground.

Later on the late Sir Arthur Evans sent me a note giving me permission to wander about his grounds at any time I wished. Again, Mrs. Marion Oliver, another friend of Lady Hosie's, invited me to stay at Tommy's Heath so that I could explore Boar's Hill thoroughly. It was during this visit that I came to listen to the Harmonious Madness.

I was not free to accept Mrs. Oliver's invitation until the middle of May 1941. I enjoyed enormously the broad view from her garden over the Berkshire Downs, though my hostess deprecated the bad weather that accompanied my visit. Irises, blue, yellow and purple, were in full bloom, and seemed to nod to me in the gentle wind as if to welcome me as a temporary guest to the garden. Only a temporary guest! No matter whether one could live a hundred years, or even five hundred and fifty, as a modern American scientist suggests, one would still be a temporary guest in the garden of the world. I was eager to express my gratitude to the irises, so I went round the garden and gave greeting to each one. Some replied with a broad smile, but some of the more timid ones were too shy to smile and hid their faces in their tiny leaves. Their heads swayed and nodded with joy as though blown by the wind, and I felt happy too. In one of the flower-beds I noticed the crimson faces of peonies peeping out to watch me, so I gave them a warm greeting in return.

Before darkness fell completely a tiny blue-tit flew down on to the lawn, hopped across the grass, and flew away into a small hole between two stones in the low wall of the terrace—a natural nest already made for him and his family. How intelligent of the little creature to find and make use of it! It must have been his bed-time, for I was soon in bed myself.

The blackout prevented the dawn from coming into my room, so I did not know what time it was when I heard the birds singing from the trees and bushes just outside my window. I was still drowsy when the clear note of a thrush fell on my ears. Then a second bird sang, and a third, and a fourth, and I was really awake. It was difficult for me now to stay in bed, so I crept out of the house for a walk. It was only half-past six. It looked as though it had rained in the night, for everything was fresh and shining, and my eyes were dazzled by the new young green everywhere. My legs felt light and free and unattached to my body; I wanted to walk faster, even to fly. I had become a fifteen-year-old boy again.

Soon I reached the wooden gate into Youlbury Ground, and bearing in mind a notice forbidding visitors to enter without permission lest they should harm the plants, pushed open the gate and went through. My feet were almost flying along when I suddenly saw a crowd of rabbits scampering on ahead of me. I stopped quickly, but some of them had already disappeared, though I could still see some dark shadows at the far end of the path. I was annoyed with myself, for I had been careful not to make any noise in the house, but had carelessly disturbed large families of rabbits. How could I have known, though, that they would come out so early to play right in the middle of the main path? I had thought that they came out of their holes only for food and to nibble grass. Probably they had a fancy for the main path, which was well paved, and which they would have to avoid in daytime. Or were they enjoying the fresh morning air before it was contaminated by the odour of humans? I must be a reincarnation of one of their ancestors! But I have lost the rabbit's quick eye and ear to detect from a distance invisible and inaudible things.

Group of rabbits

I stood motionless, and saw one or two adult rabbits creep to the edge of the main path and suddenly run away again as if noticing that I was still there. I wished I could tell them that I was not one of those human beings who wanted to eat them and would lay traps for them in this time of war. But I had no means of making them understand me, and they had gone for good.

I moved on very slowly and came to an open space. The distant Berkshire plain stretched away to the left; on the right stood a tall pole for boy scouts in whom the owner of Youlbury Ground took a great interest.

Listen, some one was singing! I looked, but could see nobody. Suddenly I spotted a tiny dark dot in the midst of the thick grey clouds above my head. How could such a tiny dot produce that clear, varied and agreeable sound? Many modern scientists have boasted that they can achieve incredible things; but could they devise such a tiny machine to produce delightful melody, though they have made a devilish bomber to roar and kill? Only unconquerable Nature could have designed this charming little creature. We humans think we are clever enough to make use of anything Nature has provided for us, but many of us show how stupid we are by caging these birds for our selfish indoor entertainment. Their songs should be heard in the open air as Nature intended. Shelley was right to qualify this madness by the word "harmonious". I once read in a book the following passage: "Dull, indeed, must be the ear, and emotionless the temperament, that can listen to 'the Lark at Heaven's gate singing' without feeling astonished at the power and compass of the melody, and delighted at its variety and richness." I can add no more.

I was overjoyed to find that while listening to the skylark over Youlbury Ground I had reached the beginning of the rhododendron-and-azalea walk. I did not stop to question whether my plain flat face would be any ornament to the landscape or not; I was proud to stand among those massive flowers of orange, yellow, white, pink, purple and crimson, and to listen to the madly-singing lark. The peak of my enjoyment was reached when the marvellous monotonous "Cu-ckoo, cu-ckoo", and another soft note, "Cule, cule", joined in from all around. To me, knowing nothing of Beethoven or Tschaikowsky, it was wonderful music. It would have been a little disappointing and wearisome after the skylark had finished singing his varied notes, to listen to the cuckoo alone, but their combined efforts were most successful. And I must not forget the many pretty little "Cheep-cheeps" of the sparrows which hopped and flew around me.

Presently I came to the end of the rhododendron-and-azalea walk and found myself faced by a red building which I had no right to approach, so I walked half-way back and then turned down an unpaved path on the right. Bearing in mind the effect I had had on the rabbits, I walked carefully. Passing a bush and some big leafy trees, I arrived at a wooden structure like a three-storey pavilion or terrace, from which there would be a good view over the Berkshire plain. I did not climb up, partly because the pavilion by its very dissimilarity made me think wistfully of the red-and-green painted pavilions or terraces I used to climb in my own country in my younger days, and partly because the stretch of land in front, deliberately left unplanted in order that there should be a clear view, seemed unnatural.

Then I walked through a pine wood. It was dark, and gave me a chilly feeling. At the end of the footpath, at the bridge edge of the wood, I came to a small gate and a bower. The birds had been accompanying me with song all the way, and their voices were so clear and distinguishable that I sat down in the bower to listen. I am no ornithologist and cannot recognize many British birds, but the shrieking and chattering starling on the right was not to be confused with the mellow whistle of the blackbird on the left. There might have been two or three of each on different branches singing at the same time. In between came other notes from the yellow wagtail, the tree pipit, the garden warbler and the thrush. I may have mistaken the song of the thrush for that of the blackbird.

The thrush is supposed to have considerable powers of mimicry and may have been imitating the blackbird's song. But I did not really mind whether the songs were distinguishable or not; I was too deeply absorbed in the harmony of their madness. I was nearly mad myself, and had an urge to chant some well-known T'ang poems in response, as I frequently did when I climbed a hill or strolled in a wood in my own country, but I only murmured them to myself lest some other human being should come upon me and feel alarmed. I might even be sent to a mental hospital!

When I roused myself I noticed a beautiful lake below me, which I must surely have seen when I came had my attention not been distracted by the birds' songs. Only parts of the lake were visible, bright silvery patches, gleaming between the young leaves of a tall tree. How could I resist going closer!

I descended the small sandy path and crossed a wooden bridge on to the biggest of three islands, the other two of which are very small and not connected by bridges. The tall pines on this island made it look like a Sung landscape painting. Distant trees rose in the background, and weeds bordered the edge of the island. The gentle wind blew tiny wrinkles on the surface of the water, like a familiar design on a certain Chinese silk used for summer dresses. A chiff-chaff was uttering an angry cry at my presence, "Whoo-it, whoo-it", as if to order me to go away.

I then walked round the lake. The thick bamboo bushes growing abundantly near the water's edge made my hand itch to paint them. I had, as it happened, been practising bamboo-painting for some time past, and the arrangement of the long-shaped leaves of these particular bamboos would assist me greatly. There was a sudden gap in the bamboos and I saw the whole lake at once, recognizing it as the lake I had been brought to see on a previous occasion. Nature was no longer in her winter garments, but in many shades of green, red, white and blue. The red building opposite was almost indistinguishable behind the distant trees; but the massive red and pink clumps of rhododendrons in the distance could be easily detected. I was longing for some other colour to complete the picture. Suddenly a neat little bird like a goldfinch, with bright yellow wings, flew down from the tall pine on the biggest island to perch on a nearby tree. Its wings made the colour-scheme perfect at last for a painting. I had seen it at the right moment. Nature seems to have a divine power of arranging colours harmoniously as well as being able to inspire birds to a harmonious madness. In China we say that an artist must read ten thousand books and travel ten thousand miles. Reading gives nourishment to the imagination, and travelling enriches the imagination. A work of art is not created merely by imagination!

I was in contemplative mood on the way home. In the language of Wordsworth:

I heard a thousand blended notes
While in a grove I sate reclined,
In that sweet mood when pleasant thoughts
Bring sad thoughts to the mind.

To her fair works did Nature link
The human soul that through me ran;
And much it grieved my heart to think
What Man has made of Man.

Through primrose tufts, in that sweet bower,
The periwinkle trailed its wreaths;
And 'tis my faith that every flower
Enjoys the air it breathes.

The birds around me hopp'd and played,
Their thoughts I cannot measure—
But the least motion which they made—
It seemed a thrill of pleasure.

The budding twigs spread out their fan
To catch the breezy air;
And I must think, do all I can,
That there was pleasure there.

If this belief from Heaven be sent,
If such be Nature's holy plan,
Have I not reason to lament
What Man has made of Man?

I tried to compose a poem of my own without emulating Wordsworth, and my feelings were expressed in somewhat different form:

Harmonious Madness on Youlbury Ground

All around me are spring colours,
The wind is gentle and the rain has stopped.
This heart of mine is just like that of a child,
Going freely where it likes.
Suddenly I hear music in the air.
My footsteps halt, my spirit is enlivened.
Such a tiny skylark

High, high above, touches the skin of the cloud.
Turning round a hundred times its reed-like tongue,
It does not depend on any pipe or string.
Its clear tones drop like little broken jades.
Drunk with its song it enjoys itself loftily.
But who are the companions of this immortal?
The tuneful notes of the thrush must be considered;
The cuckoo's call,
With the blackbird's gossipings blend in one.
And then there are the cheep-cheep sparrows,
Hopping up and down through the young twigs.
Many grasses and weeds dance to welcome the wind;
The flowers vie in charm with one another.
I stand in smiling contemplation,
As if intoxicated, maybe looking foolish,
While nature thus reveals her wonders.
I know no joy better than this!
For the nonce I forget my weary, worrying body
And feel removed from all material care.
Others may not understand my rapture.
Why should I mind?
Life is a dream,
Its past is over and done,
There is no need to guess about its future,
Now is the time, not late, to enjoy myself.

環我皆春色風微雨住時些
心如童稚悠然任所之忽聞空
中樂止步神為發渺小告天子高
高入雲度百囀如簧舌不藉竹
與絲清音落碎玉酣歌獨自
怡誰是仙人侶和鳴數畫眉杜鵑
與黑鳥聲聲合奏宜更有啁啾
雀上下攪柔枝眾卉迎風舞群
芳爭弄姿我亦含笑立如醉
復如癡造化陳奇幻無樂勝
如斯暫忘憂患身且懷出世
思人不識我樂我何為人悲有
生即是夢往者未可追來日焉
用測行樂今不遲
遊樂百園 啞

I was back at Tommy's Heath in time for breakfast at nine o'clock, and my hostess remarked that a little walk in the early morning was very good for me. This was my first day in Youlbury Ground, and the first impression has lasted, though I have strolled there many a time since. The lake has shown me many different moods since that day.

After a week's stay I felt I knew Boar's Hill well. I took an early stroll every morning before breakfast. I walked among the hillocks and fields until I reached Oxford for lunch, and then took the two-thirty 'bus back to Boar's Hill for another walk before supper.

I feel I must thank my hostess here for being so kind as to leave me entirely free from social etiquette. I knew that my habitual silence at the dinner-table and by the fire afterwards would embarrass my hostess and her friends, so I always went to bed early. My partiality for silence has been frequently criticized by my compatriots, who have warned me that English people do not like it and that they may misjudge me on account of it, but I cannot change myself, though I have listened carefully to their advice. Mrs. Oliver, however, is a Scottish lady and does not seem to object to this habit of mine. She must have understood during my stay with her that my ears and mind were constantly filled with harmonious, harmonious madness!

11
The Wind in the Willows

MY attempts at hard work do not seem to place me in the same rank as Mr. Mole, for I am often thoroughly impatient with myself. Nor can I be classed as clever, witty, and practical like the Water Rat, though I often have the urge to compose a little Chinese song. And in my long gown I am far from comparing myself with boastful, irresponsible Mr. Toad, arrayed in goggles, cap, gaiters, and enormous overcoat, drawing on his gauntlet gloves as he swaggers down the front steps. But I agree with them all concerning the wind in the willows, and I apologize for the liberty I take in calling this chapter after Kenneth Grahame's book.

I am listening to the wind in the willows now in the Oxford Botanic Garden, where I am resting after a long walk. I found myself in the Garden quite accidentally. After lunch I did not feel in the mood for indoor work, so I set out for a walk. I went along aimlessly for a while, and then decided to go for a 'bus ride. I climbed to the top and sat in the front seat. As we entered Corn Market I saw, through the late-spring (1941) mist, the obscure image of Tom Tower, Christ Church. The mist was thinning, though reluctantly it seemed, as the sun began to gleam through, and Tom Tower was more beautiful than ever. I wanted to see more of it, so I got off the 'bus to walk to Christ Church. Now that I was in the street Tom Tower seemed to have moved farther away from me. There were bustling people and rattling vehicles between us, and the massive Municipal Buildings, though beautiful themselves in the mist, blocked my view. From the slope of St. Aldate's Street I could see only the moving heads and shoulders of the throng of people below me. Tom Tower, rising aloof above the mist, seemed to be laughing at the eternal bustle of humanity.

When a few moments later I stood at the foot of Tom Tower and could see its massive bulk rising above me, I became suddenly aware of the fleeting span of my own little life. I continued my walk, reaching Broad Walk by way of the side path where the cars of the college members are parked, so that I could look at the three little cherry-trees of which I have talked about in another chapter.

The mist had by now been driven away from the buildings, but still clung obstinately to the tree-trunks in Christ Church Meadow, almost hiding their changeable purplish-green coats. The meadow seems to vary in size according to the weather. At this time of year it appears larger than it is in reality; on a clear day I can see in detail the trees on the far side, and that brings them near to me, and makes the meadow look small.

Soon I turned to walk through Merton Fields. The tower of Merton College chapel was gilded by the sun, and the vermilion curtains of Corpus Christi College, bright amid the yellow-grey walls and green fields, were vivid with sunlight. I directed my steps towards Magdalen Tower, rising gracefully from behind a tall tree in the centre of the field. A woman and some boys were gathering something—I could not see what—and piling it into an old cart. A perfect country scene, I thought, with an ancient city for background, and sunshine and shadow chasing each other over the fields and among the trees.

I passed several people resting on the seats along Merton wall, drowsily enjoying the spring sun after, perhaps, a sandwich lunch. The droning of the training aircraft which had accompanied me all the way, ceased for a while, and I turned to look at Broad Walk, where the two lines of tall trees stood aloof

The famous cylindrical sundial of Corpus Christi College

with an air of peace and content. And why not? How many people have complained that there is too much trouble and noise in the world! I walked on, and turning right through the iron gate leading to Rose Lane, went through another small gate into the Botanic Garden. The brightly-coloured flowers bathed in sunshine dazzled me. A small pine-tree grew on a rock beyond the weedy pond. It was like the pines our old masters used to paint, crooked and rather rugged, but graceful like a dancer. I tried to memorize it, and made a study of it afterwards.

Passing the small round pond with its lanky weeds, I strolled along inside the stone wall until I came to a group of tall trees on the path to the main entrance of the garden. I could see part of the entrance gate with its time-darkened colour and worn surface. Tall Magdalen Tower was dodging through the leaves and branches of the trees. I walked to and fro trying to get a full view, but the Tower refused to reveal itself. It was quite an amusing game, so I did not much mind not being able to see the whole of it, and became more and more amazed at its beauty at whatever angle I caught a glimpse of it.

Old gateway of Merton College

Passing through a gate I came out on the bank of the Cherwell where the sun now shone in dazzling splendour. There were no people about yet. I was alone.

Had any one been following me during the two hours I had been strolling about he might, noticing my gait, have taken me for a sick man. I like to walk slowly when there is so much to see. I sat down on a wooden seat for a rest. Shutting my eyes for a moment, I heard a gentle hissing sound. Looking up I saw in front of me, what I had not noticed before, a beautiful weeping willow, its long tassels swinging to and fro. Up and down they swung alternately, as if weaving an ethereal garment for some heavenly creature. The irises nearby nodded their heads to the rhythm of the silky willow tassels. Simile after simile passed through my mind, and now the willow tree was a huge silken duster which, in some invisible elegant hand, wiped away the dust sticking to the delicate petals of the flowers.

This leisured rhythmical swaying of leaves and flowers had an intoxicating effect on me. I became drowsy, though my thoughts were clear. I thought of willows in my own country. It is impossible to travel any distance in China without seeing willows. They are as popular as chestnut trees in England, and because of their popularity they have come to play a big part in our daily life. At the Ching-ming festival when we visit our ancestors' tombs we break off a few young willow branches to bring back home and hang on the entrance gate as a sign of spring. In far-off days when we parted from our relations or friends we waved willow branches as a symbol of the unbreakable bond between us, because the long slender branches blown by the wind seemed to cling to the departing ones and prevent their going.

I thought of the willows in Chinese literature. Our poets and writers have written countless poems and essays about them, describing them in rain, in wind, in sunshine and under the moon, or symbolizing in them their own moods. Our poets call the young willow leaf Beauty's eye, the long leaf her eye-brow, and the slender branch her graceful waist.

I thought, too, of willows in Chinese art. No good Chinese landscape painting seems complete without a willow. Our artists used to paint willows not only as a part of the natural scene, but to harmonize the picture by their grace and suppleness, to indicate wind, mist, and so on. Many of our great masters were famous for their beautiful portrayal of willow trees. We consider the willow the most difficult tree to paint, because the shape of its branches and trunk have many subtle aspects and cannot be handled by an inexperienced artist. An artist must have a thorough training in the painting of willows to become a good landscape painter. Years ago our artists used to burn the tips of young willow branches and use the burnt ends for making rough sketches on paper or silk, for the sketch could be brushed off without hurting the delicate Chinese paper or silk. Our ladies also used burnt young willow branches to darken their eye-brows... There are so many uses for the willow in China!

The following information in *The Observer's Book of Trees and Shrubs* interested me:

The weeping willow was given the name of babylonica because it was thought to be a native of the region of the Euphrates and to be the willow referred to in the Psalms. It is really a native of China, but it has long been cultivated in Eastern Europe, North Africa, and Western Asia, and was probably introduced into England during the eighteenth century. Napoleon was very fond of this tree, and its greatly increased popularity shortly after his death was said to be due to the introduction of young weeping willows raised from the tree under which he was buried at St. Helena.

Fancy: Napoleon liked this tree! It is no wonder that I like it so much, for it brings me a glimpse of the gardens of my distant home!

While I was deep in thought I saw a bird hopping along on the edge of the grass towards me. When it was just in front of my seat I saw that it was a fat thrush with a beautiful smooth dark brown coat. It cocked its head at me enquiringly. It had disturbed my train of thought, and I did not feel too friendly, and wondered how it was that the thrush could hop on the grass to its heart's content, in spite of the notice "Keep off the grass", so commonly seen in public gardens in England. Then I wondered whether a Chinese thrush would be allowed to enjoy the privilege of hopping on the grass. It seemed unjust that the thrush and I were both fellow-creatures, and yet he could enjoy this pleasure and I could not. From this my mind shifted to the problem of whether the written law has any effect on life at all...The thrush took no more notice of me and began to scrape in the grass. Suddenly it broke into song, and after testing its voice on a few short notes, sang a song which sounded very agreeable to my ears. From that moment it sang persistently, telling me, I thought, how rough and cruel the human creature is, and how different from a bird. He and his fellow-birds would do the grass no harm, he assured me, but a man's heavy feet and careless behaviour would certainly stop it from growing. That was why the notice applied to humans only. Human beings thought themselves too clever to trouble about many things, but they were really very silly creatures, and had always misused their wisdom. Why, human beings had such an extraordinary mentality that they would even kill each other! Look at the war...

On pondering this interpretation of the thrush's song I felt ashamed and had decided to move when a young couple strolled towards me and the thrush flew away. We human beings are certainly callous! I got up, and on reaching the gate by which I had entered realized that I had made a complete circle of the garden. Normally I should have gone out through the gate towards Magdalen Tower in High Street without sitting down at all; or, if I had walked straight on when I entered the garden from Rose Lane I would have passed the willow first. So it had all come about by chance.

On my way back to Rose Lane I kept turning to have yet another look at the swaying willow in the wind. A few people were playing tennis beyond the tree, and I wondered whether they too had seen the grace of the willow branches. A familiar story came into my mind: The Judge of Purgatory decided to send one of his spirits back to earth in the person of a rich man, but the spirit refused to be a rich man and said that all he wanted in his new life was sufficient food and no worries. The Judge replied that he could provide any amount of money, but that he had not the power to bestow a peaceful happy life. Now, if the judge of Purgatory had asked *me* the question, I would have asked only that I could sometimes enjoy the wind in the willows.

12
An Unusual Companion

I LOVE rain. Even after I had spent many sunny afternoons in the gardens of Worcester College and had grown familiar with the huge stretch of well-cut lawn and the restful sleepy atmosphere, I still wondered what the garden would look like in early morning or in the rain. I may never see it in the early morning, for the college authorities do not permit outsiders until 2 p.m., but I *have* seen the gardens in the rain.

It was a mild afternoon at the end of May 1941. I had been working hard all morning on my new book *Chinpao at the Zoo*, and felt I needed some relaxation in the afternoon, so after lunch I set out for Worcester College in drizzling rain. The college porter was so surprised at seeing a visitor on such a wet afternoon that he greeted me, a thing he had never done before. Crossing the quadrangle and emerging from the short narrow path through a small gate, I found myself gazing at an expanse of fresh green, very soothing and pleasing to the eye. I was the only visitor, and the garden seemed much bigger in its solitude. How transformed Nature becomes in the absence of

Peony

May Day service on Magdalen Tower

Peacocks at Trout Inn

human beings! After all, a human being is only a small object of decoration in Nature, and may even be a blot on the landscape! I do not understand why so many people imagine themselves so important. Sometimes we are necessary to a natural scene, but often we are superfluous; and in Worcester College garden my sense of my own insignificance was so strong that I dared not move.

Presently I turned my gaze away in search of fresh interests. Two peonies, one a pinkish-white and the other a rich dark red, were growing near the wall on my left, proud and aloof among the other flowers. Only a few days before I had hurried to the University Park in the early morning to see for the first time this year peonies in bloom. Now, today, I saw them blooming in the rain. The rain-drops glided over the petals and slid to the ground, and the flowers looked newly washed and had a sheen on them which reminded me of my feeling when painting flowers on our Chinese absorbent paper. When my brush, filled with red or yellow colour, touches the paper, the colour is very quickly absorbed by the paper; by applying the brush in a special way, depths and gradations of colour can be effected. In the short period during which the colour remains wet it has a pleasing freshness, just like these two peonies in the drizzling rain. I derive the greatest joy when painting a flower to see the still-wet paint glistening on the paper.

As I moved closer to the peonies to smell the pleasant scent of the pinkish one, I saw a big red bud opening its tiny eye like a shy young girl in tears of joy at the sight of her love, and I composed a poem in my mind on peonies in rain:

In the midst of the gentle rain
You come out smilingly in your charming pink and dark red garments.
Why do you, angel-like faces, show special kindness to me?
Filled with emotion I must thank the East wind!

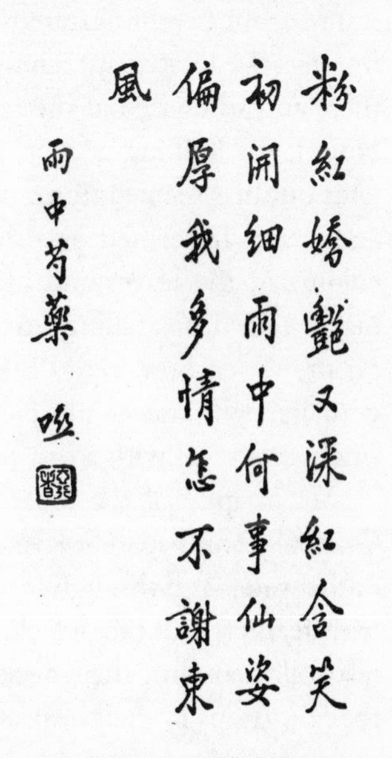

Afterwards I moved on towards the lake, or rather pond, behind the college, and watched the reflection of St. Barnabas's Church trembling, upside down, in the water. A gentle wind wrinkled the surface of the lake, and each falling raindrop made a small splash and a blob, disturbing the reflection and making an ever-moving, fretful pattern of splashes and blobs and wrinkles, while the light played and sparkled. I stood there not realizing that the rain was now heavy enough to soak my clothes, until drops from the trees began to fall on my collar and down my neck. Then I moved under the thicker foliage of a tree, and stood close to the trunk.

Suddenly I heard a coarse "quack, quack" from the foot of the tree. I looked, and saw a large bird, a member of the goose or duck family something like a drake. It had red fleshy rings round its eyes, a few distinctive black feathers on its head and a white feathered breast with black wings and tail. It seemed to be warning me not to intrude into its domain, so I hesitated to move nearer. Then I stretched my hand gently towards it in friendliness, but it showed no sign either of welcome or anger, but stared at me more eagerly. As it did not make the "quack" sound again I crept nearer and nearer until I was well under the cover of the tree. We looked at each other warily from time to time while I stood there and still gazed at the rain and the distant church of St. Barnabas. Now I was looking at it in its earthly reality, not at its reflection; the faint outlines seemed tinted with the blue-green of the surrounding trees and grass. It seemed as though the rain had dissolved some of the colours of the leaves and made the whole scene blue. Sometimes the bigger rain-drops falling from the trees by the pond made great whorls on the water. Sometimes the wind blew through the leaves, drowning with its sighs the gentle plop-plop of the raindrops. A succession of single drops fell with a distinct "di-plop" in front of me.

Yet in spite of the noise of wind and rain the scene was tranquil. Gradually a transparent layer of white vapour rose just above the surface of the water, and through it I saw in the distance a group of young swans with feathers still grey-black. One of them headed towards me and the rest followed with their necks stretched to the sky as if trying to catch the rain-drops in their beaks. They were all quite big, but they still made the sounds of young ducklings, and had I not seen them I would have mistaken them for a group of ducklings. Behind the cygnets came a pair of stately white swans floating side by side like toy boats carved in white jade, their long necks the masts. I felt that the swans and cygnets were enjoying the rain too.

I was so pleased with my afternoon that I decided to make a painting.

Before I took my leave of the pond I looked down at the big bird still standing by my side. I was amazed at his persistence and patience. He cocked his head on one side and then on the other, scrutinizing me closely and seeming to ask "Well, what do you think of the garden in the rain?" In soundless words I answered: "It's lovely."

An unusual companion, this bird!

13
It is New to Me

"ARE you going to New College?"

"Yes, I shall be there in a minute."

I overheard this scrap of conversation between two undergraduates while strolling near Radcliffe Square. In the soft late spring air a haze of peaceful antiquity seemed to permeate the very stones of the buildings. The round dominating dome of the Camera in the centre; the St. Mary's Spire; the dull yellow wall of Brasenose; the twin towers of All Souls'; the Bodleian; Hertford and Exeter Colleges—all seemed to be taking part in a solemn atmospheric ceremonial service. Two professors in long black gowns and mortar boards came out of Brasenose College, and added, as it were, a touch of *human* antiquity to the scene.

Yet there was a tinge of present-day atmosphere too: white-haired scholars in modern dress with books under their arms; a few girl students in brightly coloured jumpers and long trousers were going in and out of the Camera building; an undergraduate in khaki, evidently undergoing some sort of military training; and two W.A.A.F.s who were examining the Camera. But these products of the new world, including, I suppose, my own flat face from modern China, blended harmoniously with the ancient buildings. I can never understand why some people appear to object to the mixture of old and new: the new may even be better than the old. Even when we live in a city whose every building, almost, is redolent of centuries gone by, we cannot, save in imagination, go back ourselves.

A friend of mine, Mr. Basil Gray of the British Museum, once told me that he thought Radcliffe Square the most beautifully satisfying scene in the world; the correlation of the buildings is so perfect, he said. I agreed with him. But I have wondered whether the magnificent buildings round Radcliffe Square were designed and built at the same time and on one plan. The historians say they were not. It makes no difference; Radcliffe Square is still harmonious whether accidentally or by planned intention. I have also wondered whether it would be as attractive if no Camera was there. We can judge things only from their existing forms, and I have always thought St. Mary's Spire, in its green and spacious square, the Camera dome, Magdalen's square Tower and Christ Church's round Tom Tower, the four most outstanding features in Oxford, if not in England. The twin towers of All Souls' would have been more impressive had they not been situated so close to St. Mary's Spire and the Radcliffe Camera.

Brasenose College

Mr. and Mrs. Gray and their children, who, like me, have been living in Oxford as a result of the war, occupy a charming old house in Magpie Lane, the most famous—and the narrowest—of all Oxford lanes. They told me with pride that the landlord let them have the house because they were both Oxford graduates. No wonder *I* could not find accommodation in that ancient quarter of Oxford!

Twin towers of All Souls'

Hertford College

I turned to follow one of the undergraduates whose brief conversation about New College I had overheard. Passing under the house-like bridge connecting the two buildings of Hertford College, I entered New College Lane and approached the gates of New College. I drew a long breath and began to smile at my own stupidity, for I realized at this moment that this was the college to which the two undergraduates had referred as "New". It was an unfamiliar term to me, of course, and struck me as a little odd, for to me all Oxford was still new. But for a college founded in the fourteenth century still to be called *New*!...

Pausing at the edge of the open court with its recessed wings, I faced the garden and savoured the gentle sunshine and peace of a May afternoon. The bright geraniums in the rows of window-boxes in the wings were very decorative against the grey-yellow walls. The trees in the garden were in full leaf; standing as they had stood for centuries. The old gardener tidying up around them—a relic, too, of the past—seemed to lack the strength to move quickly, and went about his tasks as if anxious not to disturb the air.

Presently I walked along the footpath under the ancient city wall, said to have been battered by Cromwell's artillery. Perhaps, unlike our city walls in China, it has only seen one battle, for it bears no sign now of the scars of battle, and stands firm and undaunted. Having been well protected by Oxford laws and by-laws it has kept a youthful look; tiny wild flowers and velvet moss grow between the stones and on the steps. I was but one of thousands of indistinguishable visitors who had come this way and received the same welcome; but somehow—perhaps because nearly every city in my own country has a city wall, high and wide enough for large numbers of troops to march on it—somehow I had an unusual affection for this city wall of Oxford.

The flowering shrubs growing close to the wall were at their best. Some were laburnum, with bright yellow clusters hanging from the branches, each bunch like a minute paper lantern. I did not stop to identify the many flowers in the bed in front of the wall, save for the well-loved roses and tulips. Judging by their healthy look they must have been tended with great care by more than the one old gardener I had seen, who had now disappeared. Just then a pair of swallows skimmed swiftly past me, animating the stillness. What various charm this garden of New College was displaying to me! The swallows did not fly far away; they darted here and there, the speed of their movements matched only by their sureness of direction, and rested from time to time on the steps or the battlemented wall. Perhaps the wall with its resting-places had drawn them to that neighbourhood. I once heard somebody ask whether the telegraph posts were in existence before swallows! The question I asked myself was how the swallows knew of the existence of the wall round the garden of New College.

By this time a few visitors had appeared. Some were sitting on the wooden seat on the edge of the lawn, a rich green velvet carpet, which sloped down to a hollow centre. Two were standing discussing, surely, the weather or the flowers. I stepped back a few yards to get a general view of the scene.

The fencers

At intervals along the old city wall were semi-circular recesses, looking from the outside like round towers, and providing, within the garden, ideal places to sit in contemplation. I sat down on the iron seat in the last recess almost at the end of the footpath and sheltered by a huge chestnut tree. I closed my eyes, picturing in my mind the beauty of the garden.

When I opened them again, the view before me was completely free. Through the branches I saw two white-clad figures fencing, one of whom was evidently the instructor. I have always liked to watch the graceful movements and artistic poses of the exponents of this art, but alas, fencing is rarely to be seen nowadays. The Chinese mode of fencing differs from that of the West, but the two have fundamental similarities. I watched these two swordsmen with interest. The pupil, by twisting himself into unusual postures, made an awkward opponent, it was clear, and there was consequently much laughter. What a happy time of life are the college days!

I crossed over to watch them more closely, and I could see now the wire masks over their faces, a necessary precaution, no doubt, but one which spoilt the grace of the movements.

Continuing my way I discovered, at the corner near the college wall, a group of green bamboo leaves nodding their heads to me in the wind. They must, I thought, have recognized my racial kinship with them! The wind swished pleasantly among the trees, yet still the garden was silent and peaceful. How could I fail to be moved to put my thoughts into verse?

清幽美景佳遊踪學
院稱新古色濃半醉
半醒春五月雜花齊
放滿園紅
新學院花園
啞

The fresh and tranquil scenery has checked my wandering feet,
A college called New is full of antique colours.
Half drunk, half awake, oh, the spring in May!
A thousand flowers in bloom redden the entire garden.

14

Toast to the Morning Mist

I HAVE an old book called *Living London* which I picked up in the Caledonian Market five or six years ago. It is edited by George R. Sims, who was, I am told, a very popular journalist in the earlier years of this century. By an odd chance the book escaped destruction in the bombing of my London flat, and, reading it one evening in Oxford, I came upon a passage about the canals of London and the curiously-named craft—"Monkey boats" and "Fly boats"—which ply upon them. What could they look like? And what was the procedure called "legging" by which, apparently, they were conveyed through the long canal tunnel? There was this paragraph:

> *A stagnant waterway, on which slides a narrow, slender "Monkey boat" drawn by a horse that occasionally gets his head down at so much collar work. In front of the animal a budding bargee (he ranks as fourth mate—or fifth, or sixth) with a fine display of shirt-sleeve and a gift of repartee never allowed to lie dormant when the tow-line gets crossed. Now and again he makes a flick at a fly on the horse's "near" ear, thereby hurting his charge considerably more than the insect. In the stern of the boat, behind the entrance to the cabin, on top of which a caged throstle pours out a ceaseless song, and partly hidden from view by the dog-kennel—perhaps a soap-box or an old caustic-soda tin—a buxom female whose russet face is framed in a print sun-bonnet of the "truly rural" pattern, her hand on the tiller, her eyes generally looking ahead, as a good steerswoman's should.*

Before I came to Oxford this paragraph would have meant nothing to me. I lived in London for more than six years and never once saw a Monkey boat or a Fly boat on any of the canals. But the very first time I went for a walk along the Oxford canal my eyes identified, near the bridge which leads to the G.W.R. station, a long-shaped boat at anchor by the bank. I liked the bright paint on her sides, and walked over the bridge to get a closer look. I read the name of a coal company, like a kind of shop-sign, on the hull. Inside I could see a crowd of clean and shining domestic utensils and an oil lamp. There appeared to be nobody on board. I thought of the "house-boats" on Chinese rivers and lakes: it seemed to me that there was much in common between them and this Monkey boat. Our house-boats, however, are bigger, and are used not only for carrying goods but for pleasure trips.

I recalled the most enjoyable trip I ever made on a house-boat. It was along the canals to Lake Tai in Soochow some twelve years ago. With three friends I hired a house-boat for a month. There were two cabins, one big and one small, the small one being occupied by the boatman and his wife and their five-year-old daughter, while we four friends sat, ate and slept in the front cabin. At night we spread our blankets and sheets on the floor, beneath which was the merchandise for the different villages at which the boat would be calling, and rolled them up at dawn. The boatman rowed steadily on all day, and we watched with rapture the ever-moving riverbanks. Sometimes we helped to paddle. Sometimes we got out to walk along the bank, or to tow for a while. Sometimes we watched flocks of wild ducks winging across the horizon. Sometimes we searched for herons—white dots among distant reeds—which at sunset looked very beautiful in the reflected light. Sometimes we fished and caught a few.

I thought again of Soochow, a flat country where the canal is bordered on both sides by rice-fields. For days on end one may not see a living soul on the banks—just the haze of young green rice stretching away until it meets the blue sky. To reach a small village and see busy villagers was a welcome break for us, especially as we could then obtain fresh meat, vegetables and fruit. Our boatman's wife was an excellent cook.

The woman on the Oxford canal boat may have been an excellent cook too, but I gathered that there would be no room here for pleasure-seekers. I had not felt satisfied with just seeing the boat at anchor; I wanted to see it moving. The canal seemed too narrow for the boat, and I longed to see how it glided along the winding waterway past fields and trees and buildings. So for a time my figure was to be seen frequently on the tow-path. Morning and evening, in rain and sunshine, I wandered there. Sometimes I saw a fisherman looking at his catch with pride, but, though I enjoyed watching him, I still hankered after the boat. Finally I decided to give up my vigil; the things we most want often come to us suddenly, when they are farthest from our thoughts.

The climate of Oxford is not very different from the rest of England. Yet the heavy morning mist over the canal on summer mornings seems to belong to Oxford alone. I have developed a liking for this weather. When I wake up early and see the sun beginning to gleam through the mist I like to walk along the canal-bank before breakfast. On one of these walks I reached Aristotle Lane without seeing a soul. I walked slowly northwards from the bridge, in a morning mist so dense that I could scarcely see before me. On one bank of the canal are fields adjoining the railroad, and on the other nothing but back gardens. Always a few yards ahead of me the canal-banks seemed to end in some mysterious manner, yet as I walked they opened out again. In fine, clear air the canal-banks might have appeared to me in all their sordid detail, but in the misty morning everything was transformed. A profusion of flowers grew in the back gardens of the houses, and their different colours tinged the shroud of mist with blobs of yellow, green and red, as I have seen elsewhere only in London parks. As I walked along I would see one of the blobs grow deeper in colour and a rose would stand out clearly on its slender stem as I passed, like a charming girlish face peeping out between pale-coloured curtains, shy but with graceful dignity. It was at such moments that I realized more vividly than ever the cunning of our great masters who would paint only a few flowers, gracefully arranged, and give a masterpiece to the world. What more is needed?

Presently I heard an intermittent "quack, quack" from the dense mist. A number of white ducks appeared coming towards me, the purity of their snowy feathers enhanced by the grey of the mist. Even their whiteness showed different tones from one to another as they came out.

Their brownish beaks and dark red eyes seemed to have been perfectly designed by Nature for such a setting. Gradually I could see more and more clearly the stealthy movement of their brown feet under the water. The leader, with his neck stretched out in lordly manner, quacked incessantly, and the others followed, quacking at intervals. At first they had not seemed to be moving very quickly, but soon they appeared to vanish in a twinkling, speeding on like a white-shirted racing crew. The mist and the dark green water, still as death before, had been brought to life. Although I must confess that on the Thames I have always thought white swans more beautiful than white ducks, which seem so small on the wide expanse of the river, yet here on the Oxford canal the ducks take on a new significance.

Farther along was a windmill and, on both sides of the canal, school football grounds. Occasionally I met cyclists on the way to work. When within sight of another bridge leading to Wolvercote, I turned back, still with the same refreshing sense of leisure. Nothing could hurry my steps, not even the knowledge that breakfast was probably already on the table. I had feasted already on the beauty of the morning and the thinning mist. The tall chimney of a factory was hidden behind a poplar tree whose leaves swayed gently in the breeze. I could see the faint pinkish roofs of houses, and in the distance the spire of St. Philip and St. James's church emerged, aloof and indistinct. A small wooden bridge silhouetted against the sky brought back the memory of Van Gogh's famous painting "Broken Bridge".

I wanted to climb the bridge, but my feet refused to carry me farther until I had filled my eyes with the fresh view on the opposite bank, which I had discerned on my outward journey only through the mist. The long grass on both banks of the canal formed two parallel green lines cut by the clear reflection of clouds on the water, until both grass and clouds met and merged at the bridge.

While I was gazing I suddenly heard "pomp… pomp… pomp…" behind me. I turned, and saw-what I had been longing to see—a long, slender boat gliding down the canal! The boat's bow was covered with rags, beneath which I guessed coal was loaded, and her stern was brightly painted like her sides. At the rudder, his eyes fixed ahead, was an elderly man, instead of the buxom female of *Living London.* The small dog standing on top of the little cabin in the stern barked now and then as if to announce their arrival. The boat was propelled, not by a horse on the tow-path, but by a small motor. Behind it, moving even more slowly, came a second boat, then a third tied to the stern of the second. There were several people on board busy drinking their morning tea, and looking fresh and happy. Perhaps they were glad to be in sight of their destination.

Climbing on to a mound of earth, I saw the whole scene at last in detail; the boats, the bridge, and the distant church spire. The first boat grew gradually smaller and its bright paint fainter as it approached the mist-bound bridge and vanished into some unknown part of England. Two figures stood on the roof of the last stern-cabin with their tea-cups in their hands, and I thought they must surely be toasting the morning mist. When all three boats had passed under the little bridge and disappeared I continued homewards. The white ducks were now on the far bank of the canal, many of them asleep. I felt content with my walk, and raising my hand I, too, toasted the morning mist.

A common sight

15
Honourable Pussy Cat

IN my eight years' residence in England I have seldom been to the cinema. Not that I dislike the pictures, but most of my time is taken up with "silent travelling"—or, to be more exact, silent walking—when I am not engaged in painting or writing. I have, however, become familiar with the names of several film stars; Charlie Chan, for instance. It is four or five years since I saw him on the screen, and I have quite forgotten what he looks like, but I have been reminded of him more than once since I came to Oxford.

One summer evening while it was still light I was travelling on the top of a 'bus to Carfax. In front of me were four schoolgirls talking noisily, one of whom, a child of eleven or twelve, kept turning round to look at me. Then she would say something to her companions who would look round too. I could not hear what they were saying, but no doubt they were interested in my face being flat and strange. When we reached Carfax the girls alighted in front of me. No sooner had I stepped off than one of them shouted "Charlie Chan!" and the others followed suit. I presumed they recognized me as a fellow-countryman of Charlie Chan, so I smiled my thanks, and most of the passengers smiled too.

A few weeks later I was walking along Abingdon Road to visit a friend. Before reaching Lake Street I met a group of girls and boys coming from the swimming-pool. Suddenly one of them exclaimed "Charlie Chan!" and then "Look! Charlie Chan in Oxford!" I wanted to stop and ask them what they meant, but they had gone. When I reached my friend's house I told him that I was now known as "Charlie Chan". He smiled, and after scrutinizing me in silence said, "You do look like Charlie Chan, you know," and we both laughed.

Eventually I discovered that the old film "Charlie Chan in Panama" was being shown at the Scala in Oxford, and obviously some of the boys and girls must have seen it. In order to see how much I really did resemble Charlie Chan I decided to go and see the film too. He proved to have a face as flat as mine, but his broad cheeks and forehead made his face square, while mine is more rectangular. I could imagine, however, that in profile, had I his moustache, we should look pretty much alike, and I was not surprised at the children's mistake. Most English people think that Chinese all look alike, but they might find it hard to believe that when I first came to England I found it difficult to distinguish between English faces!

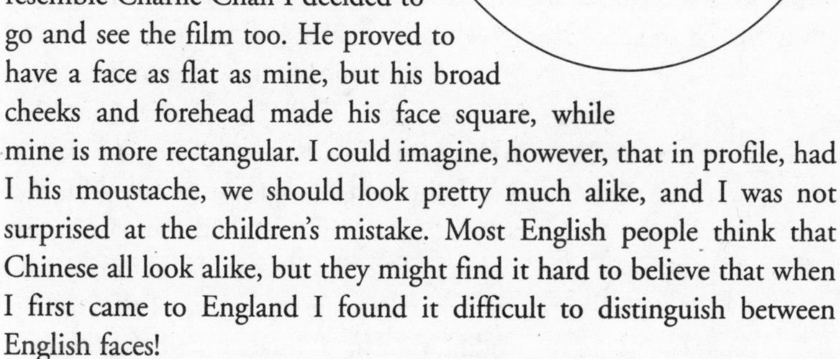

Charlie Chan and myself

I was deep in thought and not really attending to the film when the audience burst into laughter. I looked at the screen. Charlie Chan's son had followed his father after dark to search a large house and was disturbed by something jumping from a height. He told his father it was a pussy cat, but Charlie Chan corrected him, saying "*Honourable* Pussy Cat". The audience was apparently laughing at the idea of addressing a cat as "honourable", and I laughed too.

I seem frequently to have heard that word "honourable" in Oxford. It may be due to the scholarly manner of the Oxford dons and undergraduates, who are always most polite, or perhaps it is the custom to address others as "honourable" in formal debates.

I have heard the word used at the debate meetings of the Oxford Students' Union, although here, where I have occasionally been invited to meals by friends, the suave Oxford politeness seems to be perhaps less noticeable than formerly. Apart from the excellent cooking, what interested me most was watching Oxford old boys walking slowly about the building. Some of them found it difficult to see, and some were bent with age; but all still wore their worn-out college gown and frayed top-hat or cap. They looked the gentlest and most polite people in the world. Now and then one of them would get up to look at the papers and magazines on the table, but his bad eyesight impeded him and disturbed the others round the table. One would sink deep into the armchair beside the fire and snore loudly. Then some one in khaki would tramp across the floor in heavy boots to look for something. Chattering noisily round the fire, their backs to the room and only their legs and arms discernible, a boy and girl, both undergraduates, would be immersed in conversation. I liked seeing these people at the Union, and always seized the opportunity when I was asked to go there.

"I want some salt—salt"

I had not found time to listen to a Union debate until our Ambassador, Dr. Wellington V. K. Koo, came to take part in one. I obtained a ticket from a friend for that evening, and had tea and dinner in the Union before the debate. While my friend and I were having tea in one of the upstairs reading-rooms, a huge square figure in a black coat suddenly stood up in a corner of the room, stretched out his right arm dramatically towards the servant, and said. "I want some salt—salt." He was undoubtedly an Oxford graduate who knew the place and the servant so well that formality was superfluous. I was intrigued by a person who apparently preferred salt to sugar in his tea. What a useful campaigner the Government would find him in these days of sugar rationing!

Later I was asked to have a drink before dinner. I am no drinker, but I liked standing by the bar in a corner of the hall watching others drink. The atmosphere was not like that of ordinary pubs. The customers talked about politics incessantly. A few made gestures as if playing golf.

Peaceful lake in Youlbury Ground

Worcester College lake in rain

These budding politicians and sportsmen in their brightly coloured pullovers and scarves were interesting to observe and sketch. Suddenly some one broke a glass, and a burst of laughter came from a small group round the bar.

When we were finishing dinner a fair-haired young fellow came to our table and unceremoniously dragged away the waitress who was making out our bill. He did not speak, but pointed with his finger to the middle of a silver or copper plate in her hand while she was moving to another place. I chuckled at his persistent and unperturbed manner, but the diners in the hall were evidently accustomed to him and took no notice. Even the waitress did not seem to mind.

To my surprise, it was this young man who, after the Union meeting had been opened by the President, spoke first. I was sitting high up in the gallery and could not hear very clearly what he said, but from the laughter that followed another young speaker, who was supporting the first (on how to advise the Union Cook to get rid of flies in the food, or something of the sort), I assumed that they were discussing Union "private business". At last it began, and each speaker warmly praised our Ambassador and all my countrymen for their courageous resistance to the Japanese invaders for five years.

Union debaters

Becoming suddenly self-conscious about my racial identity with the people being so praised, I shifted slightly in my seat, as if in acknowledgment. My feelings, however, were far from being unmixed gratification. I have recently heard and read similar praises at public meetings, in the press, and in private conversations—and always with gratitude for the honour and courtesy thus done to my people. But sometimes—the present was one such instance—I ask myself if we wholly deserve it? How often do *we* praise the British? A few of us, who happen to be living or to have lived in England, know what a valuable example the British people have been to us, and hold in genuine admiration their firmness, perseverance, courage, thoughtfulness and kindness. Even when in straightened financial circumstances themselves, they can raise a war relief fund for China.

I am constitutionally the reverse of hot-headed; I am naturally disposed to place my trust in facts rather than in emotional attitudes. I appreciate sincere praise, but I feel apprehensive when it is divorced from honest criticism of weaknesses. And China, after all, is a very "young" nation in the modern world, though very old in the history of civilization, and it is obvious that she has faults, some even serious and dangerous faults. (What nation has not?)

It is sad that praise of China should be confined so exclusively to the toll of lives laid down in this war, of property sacrificed, and endless suffering. It is sadder still for me to see compatriots who, by whatever chance, have, like me, not themselves suffered the worst afflictions, swelling under the showers of vicarious praise, and boasting. The war is not won yet, and present praises are for sacrifices already made and accomplishments already complete.

I cannot help recalling that in China's unregenerate days, during the beginning of the Revolution, when praise of her was rare, there did in fact exist among her people many time-honoured virtues that are now all too often conspicuous by their absence. Many of us of the present day have so frequently failed to express ourselves amicably and to behave according to propriety in the conduct of life. True, these weaknesses are partially excusable in a most troubled period like the present, when parental training is at a discount, and indeed when few parents can themselves look back upon a seriously guided youth. There is, of course, the training of the schools; but schools exist primarily to instil knowledge and to provide the tools of thought; they have little time or (seemingly) inclination to teach pupils *how* to live. It remains true that the new young China has much to learn from the West, ethically, as well as scientifically.

In that post-war world which we all so fervently believe will be orderly and peaceful, I like to hope that each will have his due and be accorded the regard, and treated with the respect, appropriate to that station and its significance in the community. But I sometimes doubt whether those who are now so energetically planning and discussing the great reconstruction allow such considerations to weigh with them. To me they are a more important means of securing a lasting stability than even the provision of income and a "high standard of living" for all.

But I have digressed too far from my subject.

Dr. Koo now rose to speak.

Then followed a number of speakers. What struck me most was the frequent repetition of such phrases as "Honourable gentlemen of this side and of that side", and "Honourable members of this house". I was astonished at the exaggerated gesture of the speakers in saying these words. The mention of the word "honourable" reminded me so vividly of "Charlie Chan in Panama" and the Honourable Pussy Cat that I rather lost the thread of the debate.

Union debaters

I must not close this chapter without mentioning a stout speaker who appeared to assume Mr. Churchill's manner and imitate his voice. He was most impressive when he said "Mr. President, Sir" or "Honourable Gentlemen, sir" as though blowing out a candle. With his head bent forward over his notes he might have been Charlie Chan bowing to the Honourable Pussy Cat, for I could not see his face clearly from my gallery seat. I laughed to myself and murmured: "Here *is* Charlie Chan, Charlie Chan in Oxford." After all, Charlie Chan was a westerner.

I still smile when I think of that occasion.

16
Mercury is Quiet

I HAVE looked round Christ Church many a time. Two things impressed me particularly in this College: the famous kitchen, and "Mercury", the little formal pool in the middle of Tom Quad.

I have seen the hall of Christ Church and had tea in a room occupied by an undergraduate friend of mine in 1936. I was recently taken by friends round the cathedral, and saw the library and other historic buildings. I have also walked up and down the staircase to the hall in order to look at the pattern of the famous ceiling, and strolled to and fro in the cloisters. These should have impressed me very much. I had heard a great deal about them before I saw them; many friends had told me of their beauty and historic connexions; I had read endless adulatory phrases about them in guide-books and books on Oxford. What can there be left for me, a humble Chinese who has not the good fortune to be a member of this famous college, to say about them? A Chinese proverb says: "Things, if rare, become precious," to which I may add: "Things, when too familiar, are unnoticed." Perhaps I was too familiar, in advance, with these objects in Christ Church. More probably my feelings are due to my being an odd person who indulges himself by taking pleasure in things not noticed by those of a more objective turn of mind.

It makes me smile to read in books on Oxford such expressions as: "Here is the new part, not wholly hideous," or: "There is the uninteresting new junction," or: "A modern restoration, however

Staircase to the hall, Christ Church

faithful, is always apt to be a little disappointing." Such writers naturally place a high value on the *age* of the Oxford buildings. Personally, I am never able to see that age makes any difference to the beauty of a work of art. History only adds colour, a *patina* of antiquity, which has its charm but cannot change intrinsic merit. All new things eventually become old. I like to see things as they are and to leave names and dates and the endlessness of historical associations to the historians and archaeologists and antique lovers!

The kitchen of Christ Church appeals to me perhaps because "the kitchen front" is one of the most-talked-of topics nowadays. The more food is rationed the more one's mind becomes obsessed with the kitchen. I should not myself have known much about kitchens had I not come to live in England; it was only after I had been here a year that, fancying a Chinese meal from time to time, I started to learn to cook for myself.

The first winter I spent in Oxford I eagerly sought the kitchen. It was about the time of the Chinese New Year (we Chinese have adopted the Gregorian calendar, but most of us like to keep the festivals according to our old calendar). Three of my compatriots who were living in Oxford at the time suggested buying some pork for a Chinese dinner, and the four of us went into the town and queued at the market for hours. In vain. That New Year Festival of ours passed without pork for dinner; we used other meat instead. I had just read about the ex-premier, Mr. Lloyd George, keeping 500 pigs on his farm, and I painted a picture of Farmer Lloyd George consulting with his pigs whether they could spare a little pork for us. This was only my fancy! A number of my English friends have expressed to me their dislike of pork, but I notice that they take bacon and ham quite willingly—as if bacon and ham came from some other animal than the pig!

Now let me write about my visit to the kitchen of Christ Church. The credit for this pleasant evening must go to my friend Noel Carrington. He and Mrs. Carrington came to spend a week-end with me at Southmoor Road, and after tea we went for a walk in the town. The curious names of the little streets—Logic Lane, Blue Boar Street—seemed quite familiar to Noel. Passing through a big wooden door we were greeted by a most tempting smell. A bright light was concentrated upon a young cook frying fish in a large pan. On a shelf were huge silver saucepans, silver dish-covers, big silver plates, forks and spoons; at least, I assume they were made of silver, for they gleamed and sparkled beneath the electric light. The reflection lit up the rest of the room, revealing a huge space. The vast dark chamber looked mysterious, but my eyes were riveted on the enormous fire-place, which seemed to me much bigger than the one at Parcevall Hall, of which I spoke in my book *The Silent Traveller in the Yorkshire Dales.* The fire-place at Parcevall Hall would have held a divan bed, but this one in the kitchen of Christ Church would easily have held a double bed. Appropriately, the owner of Parcevall Hall is a graduate of Christ Church. But he did not copy the Christ Church kitchen in his own house, for Parcevall Hall was in existence before the Tudor period when Christ Church was built. Mrs. Carrington told me that the kitchen at Christ Church had been famous for its spaciousness, and its pans and plates, for centuries.

While we were chattering, an old chef in a white uniform, obviously in authority, appeared and unceremoniously shouted at us: "Do you know that this kitchen is closed to visitors?" I felt awkward and turned to go, and even Mrs. Carrington was embarrassed and urged Noel to come away. But Noel remarked calmly that he was an old student of the College who might surely be permitted to show his friends round. "Oh, all right, then, go ahead," the old chef replied, and moved to another part of the kitchen. So we had a few minutes' grace. Before leaving I had another look at the huge fire-place, which unfortunately contained no fire, and at the shining pans and plates. How many times have my thoughts returned to it since!

Once I mentioned Christ Church kitchen to another great friend of mine, one who is always dressed very neatly and moves and talks very much according to the rules of propriety. He also is a graduate of the college, and when I mentioned the kitchen he raised his right hand and adjusted his tie for a moment before replying. I may be wrong, but I think this little mannerism is a characteristic English gesture of pride. My friend told me that the kitchen was the first part of Cardinal Wolsey's buildings to be finished, a fact which has always been a source of witticisms. He also quoted the following Latin epigram:

Egregium opus! Cardinalis iste instituit
Collegium et absolvit popinam,

which somebody translated:

Here's a fine piece of work! Your Cardinal
A college plans, completes a guzzling hall.

Christ Church people excuse the matter by saying that this is quite in the Oxford tradition: good living regarded equally with learning. The building is, of course, quite unique, a piece of corresponding magnificence to the hall, with its line of fine portraits.

An American visitor once asked jokingly whether the kitchen was a purely literary establishment or was it possible to get a snack there? In my opinion Cardinal Wolsey was wise and human to build this part of his college first. It is said that he had only finished this part when he lost the King's favour and was prevented from finishing the building. Had he started to build the other part first, he might not have been so well remembered now! After all, food is the most important factor in human life, and why should college students not have a good kitchen? I do not know any stories connected with food about English students, but well-known scholars of my country have invented special dishes named after themselves and have written elegantly on the subject of elaborate cooking. Some have even said that if a student could not have the best food, inspiration in mental work would flag. It may be that Christ Church students in the past indulged themselves in the "guzzling halls" and became so conscience-stricken that they aimed witticisms at Cardinal Wolsey.

I wish I could have seen the huge joints of meat roasting on spits over the great fire. This kitchen must have served many important

Englishmen who have since helped to shape English thought and life. Great men of England, your brains must be fed with good food! Do not let this splendid kitchen be deserted and so starve the brains of your future heroes!

Perhaps, however, I am a luckier man than the American visitor, for I *have* tasted *something* from this kitchen. One day Professor and Mrs. Hodgson kindly asked me to lunch with them and Mr. Blackwell (of Blackwell's bookshop) at their quarters in Tom Quad. The lunch was delicious, and I liked to think that the dishes must have come from the great kitchen. Even as I write, I can smell that beautiful smell of cooking.

It was during my visit to Christ Church with the Carringtons that I first saw the small round pond in Tom Quad called "Mercury". We had just emerged from the main entrance when Noel suddenly had a whim to talk to the old porter of his "mother-college" (a Chinese expression). This provided me with an excellent opportunity to watch the typical Oxford manner and hear their peculiar "Oxford" conversation. One asked about a particular notable person who had once studied there, and the other answered that that was just before his time and that he had come to the College "only" twenty years before. Then they talked about a certain professor who had apparently had somewhat strange idiosyncrasies.

"Oh, him. He is still here."

"He must be getting on, surely!"

"He still has his peculiar habits, you know. He still walks very fast and bangs into the wall!"

"I remember his eyesight was bad."

Occasionally they laughed. In the end the old porter remarked, "Mercury is quiet nowadays." Noel explained to me that the students sometimes drank too much and had been known to fall into the pool at night.

Since that day I have strolled round Mercury many times. It is not that its shape is at all remarkable, nor is there anything extraordinary about the little figure—a statuette of Mercury, I believe—in the middle; it is the goldfish and other fish that I like to watch. In rain, in wind, or in sunshine, they are tranquil and happy. The spots of rain on the

The statue of Mercury

surface might, one would think, deceive them into thoughts of insects and other food, but they never appear to get excited. The ripples caused by the wind may occupy their attention, but not for long. When the sun shines the flat silvery surface looks exactly like an ancient Chinese Han bronze mirror with a lid. The white, red and dark blue colours reflected on the scales of the fishes provided a beautiful "decor" for the mirror. The bigger fish do not seem to move much. They lie at the bottom, with their fins flapping steadily. The smaller fish are not quite so still; when they move, they turn quickly at the first stroke and then glide on with smooth and easy grace. The very small fish usually play together in groups. They dart here and there in quick and supple movement, never colliding. They have a calming effect on their audience, for they take life easily and never pant or sweat.

This small pond is conveniently big for the fish to sport themselves in. Though their world is small, they seem a very homogeneous and harmonious community. Do they ever quarrel? I do not know, but in connection with them I like to think of our great philosopher Chuang Tzu, who, with his friend Hui Tzu, was crossing the bridge over the river Hao when he exclaimed how happy the fish seemed, swimming about so gracefully.

"You are not a fish," remarked Hui Tzu. "How do you know they are happy?"

"You are not me," Chuang Tzu retorted. "How do you know that I do not know that the fish are happy?"

"Very well, I am not you, so I do not know you," Hui Tzu replied. "But still you are not a fish, so it is obvious that you do not know that fish are happy."

"Let us return to our original point," Chuang Tzu pursued. "You asked me how I know that fish are happy: that means that you already knew that I knew fish are happy when you asked me. I *know* the fish are happy in the River Hao."

Fortunately I have not so far met a friend who would argue with me thus about the fish in Mercury. If the fish are not happy there, I doubt if I would be so content to watch them. I begin to wonder whether there were not fish in this pond when it was first built. The spaciousness of Tom Quad enhances my feeling of content.

One evening I had coffee with the Hodgsons. Another friend of theirs, Mrs. Ernest Milton (Naomi Royde-Smith, the well-known English novelist), who was present, told me that she had been reading my book *A Chinese Childhood*. We chatted about different things, and somehow came to the subject of spires and towers. Mrs. Milton said that she did not much care for spires, because they always seemed to her like sharp knives about to stab someone. She felt a sort of inward revulsion from spires, which she thought useless as well as ungraceful; whereas, she said, towers have bells for our pleasure. Mrs. Hodgson disagreed completely. She thought the shape of spires graceful. Another guest compared many types of spires, saying that he liked some types but not others. The conversation was interesting to me, for I know practically nothing about either spires or towers.

Soon after ten I had to leave. I had not had the luck to hear Great Tom, the bell in Tom Tower, ringing as it used to one hundred and one times at nine o'clock to commemorate the first batch of students of Christ Church. It was pitch dark in Tom Quad when I left the Hodgsons, and it was raining. I did not hurry, and held my little torch to guide me to the edge of Mercury. The raindrops made no sound on the surface of the water, and it was too dark to see any fish. No one was about. It was indeed quiet. As I moved slowly round the pond, a story of a Mr. Dobby at Merton College in 1420 came to my mind. One night Mr. Dobby went out for a drink with a friend, arriving back before the college closed. While walking near the college pond, he fancied that the sky and stars were rushing down upon him, so he stepped aside to make room for them and fell into the pond. Eventually he went to bed in his wet clothes, and without knowing it slept the whole night in them. The next morning nobody knew what had happened in the pond the night before.

I am glad to say that Mercury is quiet nowadays, for otherwise the peace of the fish would be disturbed from time to time.

17
"Childlike Credulous Affection"

And with childlike credulous affection
We behold their tender buds expand;
Emblems of our own great resurrection,
Emblems of the bright and better land.

THUS wrote Henry Wadsworth Longfellow on flowers. My own particular childlike credulous affection is for buttercups. I used to see a great many of these tiny yellow flowers dotted about the London parks, but never bothered to find out their name, and I cannot even remember whether I ever saw them in my own country. Only since I came to Oxford has my affection for them been born, and it was through the action of a small child.

I read recently that—

These flowers are erroneously supposed to communicate to the butter at this season its rich yellow tinge, for the cows will not touch the plant on account of its acrid biting quality; this is strikingly visible in pasture, where, though all the grass is cropped to the very roots, the numerous tufts of this weed spring up, flower, and shed their seeds in perfect security, unmolested by the cattle; they are indeed cut down and made into hay together with all the other rich vegetation that usually occupies a large proportion of every meadow; and in this state are eaten by cattle,

> *partly because they are incapable of separating them, and partly, because, by drying, their acrimony is considerably subdued; but there can be no doubt of their place being much better supplied by any sort of grass.*[1]

It interests me to discover that the English name of this flower is connected with cattle, even if the popular belief is false.

One Sunday in May 1941, Rita, the four-year-old daughter of the family with whom I was staying, was taken by her parents to University Park with her cousin Terry, a boy of five who had been evacuated from London. As soon as she was in the park she began collecting buttercups, but Terry, in playful mood, took them from her and tossed them to his uncle, spoiling the blooms. Rita rushed to her mother sobbing: "They are for Mr. Chiang's birthday! They are for Mr. Chiang's birthday!" To comfort her, her parents and Terry helped her to collect some more. When they came home Rita gave me a big bunch of golden buttercups, and her mother told me the whole story. How could I fail to be touched? The family would not have known about my birthday, which happened to be the next day, had not one of my compatriots who lived two doors away mentioned it. How strange that my birthday should be celebrated by buttercups from so young a child! It is a long time since I left my home, and my birthdays have slipped by without my notice in the mixed stream of pleasure and sorrow that has constituted my life, and this little remembrance from an innocent heart in a strange land was unusually sweet.

Picking buttercups

Not very long afterwards Rita had ear trouble, and was in the Radcliffe Hospital for two weeks. I went with her parents to see her one Sunday afternoon. While Rita and her father amused themselves with a drawing book, the nurse told us how good she was and how little fuss she made over the treatment. When she was asked whether she had had her lunch her eyes filled with tears, and she cried that she wanted to go home because she did not like hospital food. I suggested that she should stay a little longer until her ear was quite well again, and then we could go out together to collect buttercups. She smiled at that, and we left.

The first week of June had passed, and the weather was daily getting warmer. The sun shone brightly and I suggested taking Rita and Terry to University Park to feed the ducks. Oxford. I think, is at its best at this time of the year, except to those interested only in buildings. Along the roads, especially Woodstock Road and Banbury Road, the front gardens of the houses were gay with colour, wallflowers, tulips, roses, peonies and other flowers being in bloom together, and many flowering trees, may, chestnut and laburnum, mingling harmoniously with them. I was struck with the effect of the bright yellow of the laburnum. I have always tried to avoid using much bright yellow in my paintings, thinking it would disturb the tranquil atmosphere at which I aimed; but now I know how to subdue, with yellow, the too-fiery passion of the reds and purples and bring a placid warmth to the picture.

Since living in Oxford I have heard people say that the buildings of North Oxford are hideous and repulsive and spoil much of the charm and beauty of the old city. Let them say so. I am not one to indulge in flattering utterances, and have little sympathy with showy display, of knowledge of architecture or historic beauty spots. I wonder what these people would say if they had a little place of their own in Woodstock or Banbury Road?

As Rita, Terry and I walked through the Church Walk of St. Philip and St. James from Woodstock Road to Banbury Road, I told the children to look at the little white roses on the wall of a house, but their minds were entirely taken up with the idea of getting to the park. A passer-by, an elderly lady, told me that these were the first wild roses she

The Seven Gentlemen

had seen that year, and she exclaimed, "Aren't they lovely?" I agreed, while wondering why the roses should still be called wild when they grow in gardens. There are too many things for me to understand in this world!

In the park I looked thoughtfully at the seven tall fir-trees just inside the gate. These fir-trees are among the main features of the park. I have seen them in snow. When the ground was white and the other trees bare, they stood there unchangeable, dark and upright, the personification of dignity. So I call them "The Seven Gentlemen". Now the other leafy trees and bright flowers made the park seem smaller than before, and detracted from the importance of the firs. They looked cramped, yet they retained their lordliness.

Rita and Terry wanted to rush to pick buttercups, which were still abundant, but I persuaded them to wait until we had fed the ducks.

There were many people round the small pond, some of them feeding the ducks. Rita and Terry took some crumbs out of a tiny paper bag which I held and began throwing them to the fowl. But alas, the ducks were ungrateful at this kindness, and only pecked very casually at the crumbs. "They must have had their dinner," said Rita: "I've had mine." We moved round the pond, and the children became engrossed in a duck chasing another duck round a group of water-lilies, and others floating to the little island, on which a small clump of bamboos was looking its best. It was not long before Rita noticed three ducklings fighting their way to the middle of the pond and quacking shrilly as they swam. "What a funny noise they made," she said, and stretched her lips and pulled a face as she tried to imitate it. Just then Terry shouted that there were two water-hens over in another corner. I was interested to see that the ducks and water-hens kept apart from each other and seemed to enjoy themselves each in their own way.

I could see the mother duck keeping an eye on the water-hens in case they might interfere with the young ducklings. Surely it was an unnecessary precaution, and the sort of spiteful suspicion which unhappily dwells in the minds of human creatures too. For instance, one bad-tempered individual of a certain human race hardly represents the whole of his group, but other races, seeing the bad manners of that individual, seldom fail to condemn all his fellows as a bad-tempered lot. If only I could one day see the different names of races and nations disappear from the vocabulary of mankind! Let each one of us be just a member of the *human* race, as the ducks and water-hens are of the bird race, living happily together. They do not even know that they have different names arbitrarily imposed upon them by us.

When I roused myself from my thoughts I found my two young friends still pointing out this duck and that water-hen. Fortunately they did not know my thoughts: their innocent minds were fully occupied with enjoyment. It was only I, the adult, whose mind was sophisticated... I shook them off, and turned to the bashful faces of the water-lilies scattered on the surface of the pond smiling at me as if to say that I should fill my mind only with peaceful contemplation of Nature.

I was again filled with a deep love of Nature's beauty. As though through the lens of a camera I could see the pond with its beautiful ornaments, the green island, the ducks and ducklings and water-hens, the water-lilies, and the many bright flowers round the water's edge. A few people were still feeding the ducks on the opposite side. The tall trees flanking the winding foot-paths in the distance proved an ideal background for a painting.

The three of us then walked along by the Cherwell and reached the bridge shaped like a sickle moon. Rita and Terry ran up to the top without hesitation, though it looked rather steep for small children. I tried to stop them from running too quickly down the other side, but they were enjoying the thrill of being unable to stop themselves. By the time I was starting to walk down they were up again. This time I grasped their hands tightly, and we went slowly down together. I was going to turn to the left and have a walk along the other back of the river, but there were too many people already there, sitting or lying on the grass. Lest it might prove difficult to control my young friends by the waterside, I suggested going on, and they agreed without complaint. We settled ourselves on the grass near a tall tree in the quiet field, and the children took off their coats and ran to pick buttercups.

Boats coming, boats going, full of them is the
Oxford river;
The soft paddle and light poles stir the tiny
wavelets.

Ancient and modern in Camera Square

Spring comes to New College garden

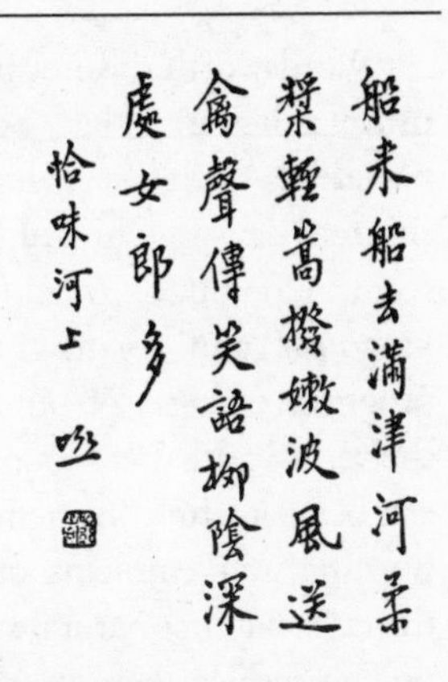

The wind carries away birds' song and happy
chatter,
Oh, in the depth of the willow's shade are many
young girls.

I sank again into thought. While standing on the bridge, I had seemed to be lifted above it high into the air, seeing the bridge below like a small silver hook clasping the centre of a long white silk belt lying curled along the ground. The silk belt was embroidered with many different boats, moored, or rowed and punted by little figures along the steadily-flowing stream. The tall trees and their branches, especially the long slender willow branches, looked like tassels on both sides of the river; and the people lying on the banks in bright red, green and yellow, were tiny dots like obscure embroidered flowers. It seemed to me a very charming picture. I nearly cried out loud that George Bernard Shaw is right in saying that we Chinese do not call English people "whites" but "pinks", for here I could verify that the flesh of those lightly-clad figures was pink indeed!

Presently Rita came up with a bunch of buttercups and asked me to look after them as she wanted to catch a little yellowish-white butterfly hovering about the flowers. I was about to persuade her not to catch this lovely little creature, but young people will not listen to words of warning and Rita dashed off across the field with Terry to pursue her prey. After all, Wordsworth had done the same thing in childhood:

Oh! pleasant, pleasant were the days,
The time when in our childish plays
My sister Emmeline and I
Together chased the butterfly!
A very hunter did I rush
Upon the prey: with leaps and springs
I followed on from brake to bush;
But she, God love her! feared to brush
The dust from off its wings.

Wordsworth did not prove a very good hunter. Would Rita or Terry prove a better? I had been skilled myself in childhood in catching butterflies with the palm or paper fan which we used on very hot summer days in China. I have read somewhere that "we almost, indeed, seem to look upon them (butterflies) as animated members of the floral kingdom, and regard them much in like manner according to the progressive stages of our lives. In childhood we long for and pursue them; in youth we poeticize them; in manhood scarcely heed them; in age begin to find in them, perhaps, alas! for the first time, sermons of warning and emblems of hope." Rita and Terry, then, were passing through the first natural stage, but I was glad all the same that they had no fans to help them. But their movements and quick steps, their merry scoldings and wranglings, among the multitude of yellow and white wild flowers, reminded me of a poem by our great poet Tu Fu of the T'ang dynasty, translated by Dr. John C. H. Wu:

Rows upon rows of flowers
In the little garden of Madam Huang!
All the branches are heavy-laden
With the countless clusters of flowers.
The carefree butterflies loiter around them,
And start dancing from time to time.
The lovely orioles are intoxicated with freedom.
"Cheerio, cheerio!" they sing.

There were no orioles here, but Rita and Terry were certainly intoxicated with freedom. So was I. We came home through Keble Road.

As soon as we got in Rita asked me to put the buttercups in a vase of water. Idly I asked her:

"Do you like buttercups, Rita?"

"Yes," she answered, very quickly. "Do you?"

"Yes," I replied, very quickly too.

[1] From *Pictorial Calendar of the Seasons,* edited by Mary Howitt, 1854.

18
Hair Raid

FOR some reason I, who live in Southmoor Road, like to have my hair cut at a little barber's shop in Abingdon Road, which is a considerable way off. My first visit was casual enough, for I had set out to see a friend who had recently come to live in Abingdon Road, and, not finding him in, I had my hair-cut in this little shop and I have continued to go there ever since, though it involves rides on two 'buses. The charge for the hair-cut is not expensive—only double the return 'bus fare—and the quality of the hair-dressing is probably nearly as good as that of the shop in the middle of the city once frequented by the more aristocratic scholars. Perhaps my preference for this little shop is due to the barber being rather deaf; he cannot make me talk while at his job.

One afternoon in July 1941, I made up my mind to go to the barber's, for I had not had my hair cut for some time and the weather was getting warmer. Unfortunately I was not early enough; there were already three customers in the shop; so I went for a stroll to see whether there really was a lake responsible for the name Lake Street.

Before long my eyes caught the gleam of a mirror-like plate hardly big enough to be called a lake in our sense. I was, however, interested to see a fisherman in a tiny boat drifting out towards the middle of it. I had thought that fishermen generally chose a pleasant spot by the river-bank, sitting by a rugged willow or hiding among the long weeds where fish were likely to gather for their bait. This angler probably knew that the fish would not approach the shore, for a railway line, with its noisy trains, ran close by, so he fished in the centre of the lake. I may be wrong. After all, a fisherman's aim is to catch fish, not to pose for an artist!

I crossed the flat wooden bridge over the lake, and stood on the arched railway bridge which joins it. My eyes travelled along the Hinksey hills on my left to the soft summer mist veiling their summit. At the foot of the hills was a row of allotments for wartime vegetable-growing. The present war has roused the English to cultivate more of their green earth, but a Chinese like me, coming from an agricultural country and belonging to a farming family, could not help but sigh at the still unploughed fields of the English countryside. On my right a cluster of dark pines rose from a grassy bank, and through the blue-tinted mist clinging to the tree-tops the famous spires and towers of Oxford were visible.

One of the charms of Oxford lies in the panoramas of its spires and towers. I like to observe and admire them in the distance from a height, though I may thus miss acquiring detailed knowledge of them. Detailed accounts of buildings are the means of livelihood of some antiquarians and historians, but why should *I* bother? My life is too short for me to remember so many unfamiliar names and historical details. I have always wished I could persuade my contemporaries not to labour to make a name for themselves, or to leave behind after their death peculiar phenomena and fanciful tales to puzzle succeeding generations.

Presently, as little sparkles of sunlight darted through the eyelet holes among the leaves and branches of the trees, a great clamour and burst of hilarity came from the swimming-pools which I had noticed on my way to Church Street. I went to see what was happening, and found a large crowd of people of all ages in scanty bathing-costumes. In great contrast to this mass of human flesh, wet and glistening in the sun, a row of lofty pines clothed in dark blue-green towered in solid strength and perfect harmony. I could not have imagined such a curious contrast and was glad to have seen it.

I walked over to a pool where only young women seemed to be bathing. Two happy and high-spirited girls attracted my attention. One, in a red costume, was an expert swimmer, and was assisting her companion, a girl in a green costume. I wondered how many known and unknown European painters would, on seeing them, have tried to portray these two charming creatures as they actually appeared. Could they be painted as perfect as they were? Or would it not be better to avoid painting a merely photographic likeness, and portray them as the products of abstract thought and imagination? For realism without imagination cannot produce a good painting.

A young bather

Watching the very young swimmers, whose ages varied between three and ten, was even more interesting. They were not really swimming, but just floundering about in the middle of the pool. Some were teasing each other, splashing and struggling. The happiest of all was a very small boy who was trying to catch a big floating rubber ring apparently belonging to his sister. I was reminded of a *Punch* drawing of an elder sister who, holding the waist-belt of her little brother, whose head and feet were below the surface, was saying "Look at baby, Mother! He's taking to it like a duck to water."

Loud shouts attracted me towards a pond beside the swimming-pools. A small black Scottish terrier was swimming round and round the pond chasing a swan. The swan looked very pathetic as, with wings upstretched, it hurried to escape from the barking terrier. The few spectators looked anxious, and children were shouting at the dog, which took not the slightest notice and obstinately continued its chase. The swan, which had the advantage of being able to fly, seemed to wait deliberately until the dog came near and then fly to another part of the pond, so that the dog was periodically left behind, and gradually began to look exhausted.

Just then a middle-aged woman, the owner of the dog, ran along the edge of the pond, obviously anxious lest the dog should drown from exhaustion, and threw a small stone at it in an attempt to bring it to the bank. There was quite a crowd round the pond, and as I had no doubt they would get the dog out, I turned away. The dog had taught me not to pursue a goal beyond my reach!

At last I reached the barber's shop again. A kindly-looking old lady was sitting near the door waiting for her husband. Smilingly she asked me whether I had come from Pennyfield. "No," I answered, "I have come from London." She seemed surprised at my answer, and I remembered then that Pennyfield was where the famous Limehouse, or Chinatown, is situated. The old lady apparently lived near there and knew or had seen many of my compatriots. She might even have a lot to tell me. She looked so unsatisfied with my reply that I hurriedly added that I had quite often been to Pennyfield. Presently she left with her husband.

While I was having my hair cut, four children, towels and bathing-costumes over their arms, dashed into the shop. Just then the siren sounded, and the children one after the other shouted out, "Hair raid! Hair raid!" until the barber told them to be quiet. The siren sounded familiar to my ears after the London blitzes, and I wondered whether it was familiar to the youngsters, or whether they were joking at my thick black hair falling to the ground in such big quantities. After all, it *was* a hair raid, and I felt not at all uncomfortable at being laughed at.

Hair raid

19
Not a Dream

ONE day my friend Wang Ke-chin invited me to lunch at Queen's College.

It is useful to have a good friend in one of the colleges, especially in wartime, for many of the colleges bear a notice: "This college is closed to visitors." Incidentally I went to Cambridge and saw a similar notice at one of the colleges, "Closed to the public". This indicates to me that Oxford and Cambridge can never be the same. But I think "public" applies locally and "Visitors", maybe, internationally. What should I, an exile and refugee, do if I wish to visit them? So Wang Ke-chin, a very pleasant fellow known to his friends as Howard Wang, who was studying comparative law at Queen's, was most helpful.

Ke-chin had also invited a mutual friend and compatriot, Colonel Chiao Shih-chai; it was, indeed, in his honour that the lunch had been arranged. The intention was to celebrate the Colonel's escape from drowning when the ship in which he set out to return to China was bombed and sunk. Although he had left Oxford for his abortive voyage only a few days before, he had much to tell us. He was full of praise for the islanders of St. Louis who had dried his clothes and provided him with a new pair of shoes. He seemed to be more elated than depressed by his experience. And why not, for had he not been granted a second lease of life?

The three of us met at the entrance to the college as early as eleven o'clock, in order to allow plenty of time to go round the college before lunch. First we went to the chapel. It was shut, so Ke-chin fetched the key and soon we were standing facing the altar in a spacious, peaceful and dignified aisle. I have no knowledge of architecture or architectural terms, but I liked the semi-circular space at the end, where the three large stained-glass windows threw a proud and splendid glory on the little cross above the altar, an impression unique in my experience. We admired the screen, the marble pillars and the great organ. Finding myself near the Provost's seat, I was filled with a childish desire to imagine myself the Provost for a moment and was about to sit down when Ke-chin, who is a Christian and had not missed a single service since he came to Queen's, stopped me.

Next moment the college chaplain appeared, and Ke-chin asked him to show us the senior common room, the smoking-room, and the committee-room. In the last he drew our attention to the many oil-paintings on the walls and related their history. I was very interested in his information about the great table in the middle of the room. It was new. The old one had had so many legs that the dons and professors constantly complained that there was no room for their own legs, and a new table was made to put a stop to the grumbling. Next we were shown an ingenious screen in front of the big fire-place. Should a professor sitting on either side of the fire-place find the fire too hot for him, he could shield himself with a leaf of the screen. But what of those *facing* the fire-place? Well, it seemed that if they also felt too hot, or too cold, all was well, for a third leaf could be drawn downwards or upwards, as the case might be. At this we all laughed heartily. What an accommodating design, and how uncompromising the minds of older scholars! I was astonished to discover that there are people in England who do not want to look at an open fire. I have since pondered further over the design of the screen. Suppose those sitting round the fire should not agree? Possibly there is a device to draw two leaves upwards together; but I am still inclined to think that, accommodating as the screen is, it cannot suit everyone's taste. One is apt to imagine that the most learned people are the most reasonable, but it seems that it is just those who think they know much and are sure of their knowledge who are the most unreasonable.

Next we visited the library. The librarian, Mr. Smith, was most friendly. First he pointed out the fine ceiling and beautiful wood-carving on the walls. I was particularly interested in the many old books piled up in the basement.

Mr. Smith showed me an ancient *Gerard's Herbal*, published in 1636, containing many fascinating illustrations.

Mr. Smith also told us much of the history of the college. When he spoke of the borrowing of books his face fell, and we all smilingly agreed that he must find it difficult to refuse to lend his books to students wishing to show off when their parents came to see them. How pleased the parents would be to think that their sons spent their money on books!

Dining-hall

At last we entered the dining-hall. I was disappointed not to hear the trumpet blasts by which the students of Queen's are supposed to be summoned to meals. Nor did I have even a small slice of the Cumberland or Westmorland ham which tasted so delicious when I was travelling in the Lake District a few years ago, though the college was founded in 1340 by Robert de Eglesfield, a Cumberland man, for the special benefit of natives of Cumberland and Westmorland. Many of our companions were in uniform, and indeed, the war atmosphere could be more plainly felt inside the college than outside it. After the main dish, which consisted of a piece of fish, came two small slices of pancake. Two young soldiers-to-be, obviously tired by their outdoor training and very hungry, finished their portions quickly and asked for more pancake. The waiter, with a forced smile, replied: "Sorry, sir. Not in wartime." We each had half a pint of beer. None of us was very accustomed to beer, though Ke-chin was more at ease than the Colonel and me. I have often wondered where an Englishman puts away ten pints or more!

As we had nothing special to do after lunch, Ke-chin offered to show us the rooms he had occupied last year. They were not in the main building but outside, to the north of the main quadrangle. Here was a real old English house. It looked as though it had been standing for centuries. The top stories jut out like those of Dickens's Old Curiosity Shop, though it has no big lattice window and is whitewashed all over. In front, a tall tree with wide-spreading branches gave the effect of an English country scene. Ke-chin opened the door and ushered us in. The small window did not admit much light and at first I could see nothing. The entrance was a winding corridor with steps here and there. Knocking on one of the doors we opened it and went into a large room with many books on the shelves and table. It was empty, the occupant being on vacation. Beyond the study we saw a tiny bedroom with a bed and one or two chairs. I was told that these rooms resembled those occupied by the students living in the main college building. On our way along the dark corridor Ke-chin opened one door after another, and we had to laugh at him as he kept saying "And here is another. And here is another." Though the corridor was dark and narrow, and the steps leading to each set of rooms rather awkward, the rooms themselves were comfortable and practical.

We went up to the next floor, where Ke-chin had occupied two rooms for a year, then on to a still higher floor. I was surprised to find so many rooms inside a house which looked quite small from the outside. In the last room, immediately above his, Ke-chin told us a story which is supposed to have been enacted there several decades ago. Living in this room were an old don and his young wife. The wife had a young lover who was murdered there by the don. It is said that the young man's spirit often returns to the room searching for his love. While Ke-chin was living in the room beneath, this one was occupied by an American friend of his called Slade, but although the two of them always worked together in the evenings in Slade's room, they never saw or heard the ghost.

The story made a deep impression on me and I hardly realized that we had left the house and had come to the college bar. The person in charge was Mr. Bert Stone, who has been at the college for over thirty years. He proved a very good story-teller. Three half-pints of beer were again set before us, but we said nothing as we listened intently to his stories. Then Mr. Stone suggested that we each taste a small glass of

"Chancellor", a special beer brewed at Queen's. He even showed us the brewery, which dates from the fourteenth century and claims to be one of the oldest in England. Colonel Chiao and I really should not have drunk any more beer, as our faces were already red, but we could not refuse this special request to taste "Chancellor", which is only offered to the members of the college on festive occasions, and the brewing of which has been suspended since the outbreak of war. We accepted gratefully, but it tasted stronger than ordinary beer, and my face grew hotter and hotter. Giddily I followed Ke-chin and Colonel Chiao out of the bar. Luckily I was able to regain my composure before we left the college.

Now that Ke-chin has been appointed to the diplomatic service in the Chinese Embassy at Washington and Colonel Chiao is back in Yunnan, and I am still an exile and refugee in Oxford, the vivid memory of our visit to Queen's has returned to me many times. Sometimes it has seemed real and sometimes a dream. Before Ke-chin flew to America, I made several attempts to obtain permission to stay for one night in the room where Ke-chin's friend Slade had lived, so that I might have the pleasure of meeting the long-unwanted lover. In vain. But I did not forget him. One morning I woke up very early, alert in a moment, though I could not understand why the oppressive darkness and tense silence should weigh so heavily upon me. At intervals there came a faint sound of footsteps walking to and fro outside, and through the little window I saw, in a feeble ray of moonlight, the dim outline of a face. At once I got up and went to the door. The darkness was still intense in spite of a pale moon, but I thought I could see, though very uncertainly, a slim figure all in black walking down the corridor away from me. When I could see him no more I turned to go back into my room, but he reappeared, this time coming towards me. I said "Hallo" several times, but he did not answer, and went away again. The next time he appeared I tried again. "I wonder," said I, "whether you would care to come in for a rest and a chat? It must be depressing to have a lot to say and no one to listen to it. Please forgive me for referring in any way to your tragedy, but I am a Chinese who has come from a far country and would like to hear all you may have to say. If you would care to confide in me I might be able to give you the sympathy you need, though I don't suppose I could help you in any practical way. But at least I can assure you that I will not repeat your story. Or you need not relate it if you don't want to. Just come in for a rest. Naturally you think yourself misunderstood by the general public. You have refused to discuss or argue the matter, because you were deprived of the right of doing so. No doubt people think you should have respected the social position of the don, but it would not occur to them that his young wife had perhaps been forced to marry him for one reason or another, and possibly he did not understand her youthful outlook and she was unhappy. People seldom care to think things out for themselves, but find it easier to accept the opinions of others. It depresses me that so many of the laws made by man are framed less to prevent wrongs happening than to punish the wrongdoers. But the people today have nothing to do with those at whose hands you suffered so keenly. The only thing they know is that they are frightened of you. *I* can understand your grief, and why you are so unhappy, but who else will trouble to sympathize with you? If you heard their remarks about your appearances here, intended as they are as a joke or to frighten someone, you would be most depressed to realize how you are misunderstood. But one is often misunderstood in life, and you must make the best of it. Confucius once said: 'He who does not feel unhappy when he is misunderstood by others—is he not a gentleman?' Cheer up, old man, if I may so address you. Come and have a chat with me…"

Before I could finish the figure began to walk away from me, and finally broke into a run. I was anxious in case I had hurt him, though I had meant to comfort him. I had myself been misunderstood! I tried to call him back, but my throat felt parched and I could make no sound. Then he vanished. I made an effort to move, for my body felt pinned by a great weight, and I awoke with a deep sigh. Automatically I switched on the light and saw to my great amazement that I was not in the room at Queen's at all, but in my own room in Southmoor Road. The piles of Chinese books on my table brought me back to my senses. Smiling to myself, I realized I had been dreaming. Then I shut my eyes again to recall the vivid scenes, while assuring myself that it was certainly no dream.

But I had, indeed, betrayed my name, "The Silent Traveller!"

20
The Bashful Face

I SHALL always remember how bashful the face of Oxford is in September. By "bashful" I mean wearing a modest, gentle expression that to me is most attractive.

In spring Oxford is always smiling; sometimes she laughs, exhilarated by her reds, yellows, greens and purples, made vivid by the dazzling sunlight. The air is filled with the chatter of birds and undergraduates. The girls particularly seem talkative; they have not the quiet gentleness of the young woman of past generations, and although they seem happy enough their minds are restless and enquiring.

In summer the city is oppressed by the thick dark green foliage on the trees, and pants for the cooling vapour from her numerous waterways. In winter Oxford sighs, for she is growing old; she weeps, for there is much rain in this season. Only in autumn, particularly in early autumn, the colleges of Oxford wear their greyish-yellow gowns and welcome with joy the mellow autumn colours that by their very beauty enhance their own quiet personality. It is this harmonious colour-scheme that gives the face of Oxford its air of bashfulness in autumn.

Not only the grey college buildings but many houses and small old parish churches lend themselves equally submissively to autumn. Even the yellow and red-brown coats of the cows and horses in Port Meadow are a harmonious part of the autumn landscape. Port Meadow, the ideal place for these animals, is quite near where I live, and I often go there for a stroll. I usually go in the early morning, for the animals are so lively then.

On the nineteenth or twentieth of September, 1941, at about eight o'clock in the morning, I paid a visit to Port Meadow. Crossing the small stone bridge from Aristotle Lane I reached the wooden railway bridge. Today Wytham Hill looked very near and low in height; it seemed that when I breathed my breath rose above it. Wytham Hill is not actually a high hill, but I have seen it in rain when, through the rain-drops and beneath thick clouds in a lowering sky, it appeared to gain in height. I have seen it when the rising mist, or the clouds severing its summit, have added to its stature. But today there were no clouds in the clear autumn sky; and I could see the hill very plainly through the sparse foliage of the trees. Distances always exhilarate with a feeling of expansion.

From the meadow footpath where I stood I could see a large group of cattle browsing in the distance. The horses which at one time used to share the field with them were now in a separate field where the Meadow begins, and were chasing each other with lively and graceful movements as if overjoyed at being at liberty in the clear fresh air. I went to have a closer look, and while walking along the outer ring of the Port Meadow allotment I found it so muddy after the heavy rain of the previous night that I had a hard job to drag my feet along. The horses, I thought, were wise to find themselves on higher and drier pasture, and I wondered where the horses and cattle went when the Thames flooded the fields.

The entire Meadow, two or three miles in length, seemed visible when I came to the heath near the group of horses. Each horse had its own individuality. Some peacefully nibbled the grass, some trotted aimlessly about, and some were still chasing each other in a line. A big brownish-black one stood, apart from the rest, as immovable as a perfectly sculptured statue in bronze or black marble. Two stood on their hind-legs with their fore-legs in the air rubbing their heads together in a friendly game, looking, in the vast stretch of meadow, like two small dogs playing. One whinnied long and loudly, and two more followed suit. The curious long-drawn sound, tailing off into silence, made no disturbance in the silence, but rather added charm to the atmosphere.

Wytham Hill, hidden behind a row of golden-brown trees by a small wooden bridge, had for the moment escaped my notice. Now, as I looked towards it, I noticed that the leaves on the trees were changing colour, and their many different shades made a delightful splash of colour, and gave me a curious feeling of depth. On the other bank of the Thames, close by the ruins of Godstow Nunnery, a group of trees, much paler in colour, were rather obscure in forms. What appears to be a long ribbon of silvery river proves, on closer inspection, to be a thick white chalk-line marking off the land; and the white and red sails gliding down the river turn out to be the little flags on the golf-course. The distant cattle might have been fallen yellow leaves; and the yellow, brown and red of the herds softly harmonized with their surroundings. The blue-grey sky had taken a greenish tinge from the autumn colours of the earth.

My thoughts went back to Port Meadow in the old days when Oxford became the seat of the English Royal family. Most historic places in England, as in China, which have become generally renowned, have some connexion with the ruler of the country. Oxford has many good reasons for its fame, but the short residence of King Charles I has proved its importance in English national life and administration. It is said that during the Civil War, in June 1644, the Parliament army set out to capture both Oxford and the person of King Charles. On the night of 3 June, the King and the Prince of Wales, with more than two thousand musketeers, marched out of the city to Port Meadow, where about three thousand horses were ready for flight. I, a Chinese, am not qualified to discuss English history, and not being an historian am not particularly interested in the detailed events of the Civil War. But I *was* interested in trying to visualize the magnificent spectacle in Port Meadow of the English King and his retinue on horseback in bright costumes such as I have seen in historical plays and in museum pictures. I saw in my imagination those mighty ones, some of the sitters at Oxford high-tables, also on horseback, with great pride keeping close to their King. The rightness of their cause would be secondary, their vanity and their desire to be members of the ruling class being stronger in them than love of principle.

It is the intellectuals who have ruled the world throughout the history of mankind. It is the intellectuals who have the ambition to rule others: right or wrong, even at the expense of intellectual hypocrisy, their craving for power is the one overwhelming passion of their

A hot argument

existence. Some of them are the cause of many of the tragedies in the lives of ordinary people. The most dangerous of our intellectuals have tried to destroy us for a whim. Our great philosopher, Lao Tzu, says: "If the intellectuals are not dead, there will be no end for the great robbers." In the long history of China we have had too many of these intellectuals only too ready to obey corrupt rulers. Great robbers, who have many intellectual followers, can bestow on them the power they crave. If the biggest enemies of humanity today had no intellectual following or support, there might have been less suffering for mankind now.

What can we expect from the intellectuals of the present and the future? Perhaps the Oxford dons and undergraduates could tell me. I am myself to some extent ruled by the intellectuals who have tried to persuade me to follow this or that "ism" but my mind is unconquerably my own. So long as I learn to live honourably and rightly I do not care for any "ism"; and it is this upright conduct of life which I expect to learn from the intellectuals of the present and the future, in the interest not of any individual or nation, but of humanity as a whole.

I was abruptly dragged from my dreams by the droning of a big bomber in training, flying just above my head. Some of the horses showed their uneasiness by a jump or other movement. The autumnal tranquillity was disturbed, so I moved on.

Seeing the bomber reminded me that the first aerial visitor to Port Meadow was in 1911, when Mr. Latham landed there at the end of his flight from Brooklands to Oxford. Then, in the last war, a training school for pilots of the Royal Air Force was erected in the Meadow, and

Homing birds over Christ Church

Swans chasing the wind over Rainbow Bridge

large numbers of aeroplanes would rise and settle there like flocks of blackbirds. What a blessing there is no training school there now! There was such peace after the bomber had passed.

It was still early, so I decided to go up Wytham Hill to see the whole panorama of the city. I had no idea how to get to the hill, but I thought I could not go wrong if I made a bee-line for it, for it did not look to be far beyond the opposite bank of the river. I did not want to disturb the horses by crossing the meadow to the wooden bridge, so I went by Willow Walk.

The willow-trees in this part of Oxford were no doubt planted for a purpose by the local authorities, for they are very numerous. Like most English willows, they have many small branches and much foliage at the top, due to severe pruning, instead of being encouraged to grow to their natural height. Here I had a new kind of willow to paint, but I have never been very happy about it because it seems so artificial. Some of the willows bordering the Walk had grown to their natural height, and the rugged and weathered trunks testified to their great age. Their big slender branches joined above my head, forming long cloisters like those of some of the old colleges. The yellowing leaves made me think of the college walls, though the daylight deepened their gold, and I instinctively lessened my pace and quietened my step as though on hallowed ground. Walking in the long dark cloisters of the colleges affects me in the same way; the low roofs and the darkness ahead seem to warn me not to disturb these awe-inspiring precincts of learning.

Just then a cyclist rode past, and I smiled to myself as I remembered a notice at the entrance to the Walk: "No bicycles on the Willow Walk." Oh, these human laws!

Soon after crossing the wooden bridge I came to the Rainbow Bridge, looking, like all other machine-made products, solid and useful. But I must say that I prefer to look at the uneven and twisted old wooden structure because it seems a part of its surroundings. The effect of the perfectly-planned metal bridge is that of forceful strength controlling Nature. Had the hills and soft green meadows been replaced by powerful rocks or high mountains, the contrast would not have been so forcible; but here, among the trees and gentle countryside, a simple wooden bridge seems to be admirable.

From among the trees with their brown and yellow foliage I could see the meeting-place of the many beautiful waterways of Oxford. The wind, so soft that I could not feel it, was rustling the branches and tops of the trees with a sound like that of the slow-running river. There seemed to be leaves everywhere, and I tried to avoid trampling on them. They fluttered gracefully and negligently to the ground like big golden snow-flakes; they rubbed gently against my cheek and were gone before I could return their caress, or touched my hands as though in greeting, and vanished. A few, carried away by the water, made their last journey to an unknown destination. Their light and airy movements were charming, and I recalled the Irish poet Forrest Reid's lines:

Slowly, one by one,
Through the damp-smelling, misty air of autumn, the delicate leaves drop down,
Covering the grass like a carpet—
A carpet woven in gold and silver—
And the sun,
Shining through the bare black trees,
Turns to a glory of gold these dying woods.

Ah! if any poet
Could stay that brief splendid vision,
Gather these autumn glories into his song,
What joy were his!
Let the winds scatter
The broken scarlet web of autumn over the world!
Soft with sleep,
Let the delicate air sigh through the naked branches,
That still preserve their beauty,
Through a barer, a more austere beauty than the green beauty of summer.

I had not realized until I suddenly looked round that I was in Binsey village. Wytham Hill, seen behind through the loose foliage of the trees, looked very near. The yellow walls of "The Perch", where I have been so many times, and the greyish-white walls and red roofs of the few village

Old Binsey Church

houses, blended well with the red and brown boughs of the trees. Some white Aylesbury ducks on a dew-pond gave life to the scene. I like autumn in England, with its masses of fallen leaves on the emerald grass, even more than autumn in China, for the dying colour of the grass in Kiu-kiang is so melancholy.

At the back of the village the trees were dense, and there were cows grazing in the fields. At the end of a footpath lined with thick grey beeches a small building was hidden away which turned out to be the charming little parish church of Binsey. I walked round the churchyard to St. Margaret's Well. I remember a young couple, friends of mine, once telling me that they had been wishing at a wishing well near "The Perch", and this must have been it. The war, alas, has separated them, and their wish can no longer be fulfilled. I wonder if it would have materialized in happier circumstances? I hope so.

Leaving the parish church, I intended going through a wooden gate on to a footpath which wound its way down the hill, but a notice saying "No Road" had been fixed to the gate and I could not pass. There was no other path to the bottom of the hill, so I waved my hand to it and promised to visit it another time.

Trying a new route for a change I walked from "The Perch" direct to Binsey Lane. One or two familiar notices in large letters —"Trespassers will be prosecuted" and the like—looked so unfriendly that I hastened on.

From the Binsey Lane Allotment I could dimly see to the right standing on Hinksey Hill the Water Tower which I was to notice again on the way to Oxford from Boar's Hill. To the left the tall erect tower of St. Barnabas was unmistakable. Far behind St. Barnabas lay the renowned city of spires and towers with the faint outline of the round dome of the Radcliffe Camera glowing in the still, clear autumn air. Spirals of blue-grey and white smoke, some curved, some vertical, rose from the chimneys of the houses and colleges, seeming at a certain height to remain stationary as though the air were cold at that height.

In China, when we see smoke rising from the chimney of a village house, we know that the occupants must be cooking, and that it is near lunch-time; but in England cooking is done much by electricity or gas, and smoke rising from the chimneys denotes a cheerful "open" fire for comfort. I like watching these slender columns coiling upwards like snakes, and was glad to have seen them in the clear ethereal air of autumn, for their beauty would not be fully revealed in cloudy English skies. I then began to visualize the glowing tree-tops round the city, and the rising smoke, as a huge fire giving warmth to all mankind. It was a lovely, rare sight indeed.

When I reached home I told myself that even if I had not been able to go up Wytham Hill, I had seen to the full the bashful face of Oxford.

21
Greetings from Birds

WHEN Mrs. Oliver invited me to spend Christmas Eve, 1941, at Tommy's Heath, Boar's Hill, to see an old Austrian Christmas Nativity play which a mutual friend, Mrs. Cornelius, was producing, I gladly accepted. Mrs. Cornelius's son Tom was to take part in the play. I knew Tom well; we became good friends when I stayed with Mrs. Oliver in the spring. Tom and his mother had been staying at Tommy's Heath for some time. We used to have exciting games in the hall after breakfast and take interesting walks in the garden. He could remember and pronounce my name remarkably well, though he was only about three. I wanted to see him take part in the play, so I set off for Tommy's Heath on the day before Christmas, after two o'clock.

Tom as the King

It was not at all like Christmas weather. The sun shone brightly on the hill-slopes, and birds flew joyfully among the tree-tops. I felt quite warm when I got off the 'bus near Jarn Mound. After a short walk I arrived at the hall in time for the play at four. The hall was really a good size, but with the little stage at one end and chairs and couches at the other, it did not seem very spacious. The audience talked cheerfully while waiting for the play to begin. Several grown-ups and six or seven children took part. Tom, as one of the three Kings, occupied practically all my attention. He has a wide smiling mouth, so that even when he was singing he seemed to be smiling. He was standing behind the Virgin, and, not being able to see what was happening in front, leaned sideways and peered round her. His smile was so innocent and happy that I made a number of sketches of him that night.

Another attractive young actor was four-year-old David Edwards, who played the part of a young shepherd. I could not see his face clearly in the dim light, but he seemed a frank and simple little fellow. He had more to say than Tom, and when his turn came he spoke slowly and firmly, and his gestures were good.

The whole production was delightful, and Mrs. Cornelius was to be congratulated on her patience in training the young actors, and her skill in not forcing their capabilities.

After the play the curtain was drawn back to reveal a big Christmas tree lit with tiny candles and hung with presents. Tom was the chief beneficiary, but he and the other youngsters were all content with one wooden fighting cock and took no interest for the time being in the other toys. By twenty-past five I was the only guest left in the hall. The days already seemed a little longer and the light was still good when the curtains were pulled to again. I sat down by the big French windows facing the beautiful Berkshire Downs. When I had stayed here before I had seen the Downs in fine weather, clad in dark blue and forming an even line against the horizon. I had seen them in rain and mist. Now I saw far below me the thick blue-black lines of each contour, the air so clear that they seemed as distant as another world. I felt my whole body expanding as I drew a deep breath. Then I noticed above the blue-black line a yellow light which soon turned to a brilliant red: sunset over the Downs. I had never before seen such a sunset in England on Christmas

Eve. A mass of dark clouds hovered above, their lower edge so straight that it might have been cut with a knife to form a line parallel with the edge of the Downs. The whole world seemed to be coloured a fierce purplish-black: the hills, the sky, and the evening mist veiling the tops of the trees. The flaming red was intoxicating by contrast, like a gaudy jade trying to appease her angry lover.

Some one in the hall mentioned blackout time, but the doors and windows were left open until the last of the sunset had disappeared.

At daybreak on Christmas morning I was awakened by the single intermittent note of a bird on the tree outside my window. It was a happy greeting, and I got up at once to return it. It was still too dark to see the bird, but I could hear the hiss of its wings as it flew from the tree, and I murmured: "Merry Christmas!" When you are in Rome, do as the Romans do. I am sure the bird understood why I greeted it in the English way.

It was still dark when I came down and drew back the curtains and sat down in my seat of the previous evening, this time to watch the day break for the first time, and on Christmas Day of all days!

Though still the Old Year, I always look upon the English Christmas Festival as our Chinese New Year Festival, so Christmas morning seemed to me now like the beginning of a new year. Thoughts crowded into my mind. I had spent eight Christmases in England, and this was my second in Oxford. I knew I must not stir up what had long since gone by, but I could not forget the recent past. What of the future? I have never been sure whether English people believe in hope or not. I have heard them say "Let's hope so", or "We'll hope for the best"; but they are wont to consider the Chinese outlook as mysterious, superstitious and unpractical. Is it not better to hope than to be merely practical? I personally would rather hope and be practical at the same time. It would be no good hoping to do a better painting next time if I could not paint at all. Nor do I "hope" for the immediate termination of this second world-war, now that fighting in the Pacific has just begun: the end is too remote. Yet on this Christmas morning I was full of hope, and glad to be able to hope in these peaceful surroundings.

Suddenly the outline of the two big trees in the garden just in front of me became clearer, and the single note of a bird sounded through the still air. There could have been no more charming greeting to announce the dawn of Christmas Day. The dark veil covering the remote Downs was lifted to reveal, not the Downs themselves, but the black velvet coverlet which wrapped them as they slept. Presently, as the reflection of the sun reached them, the hills put on a blackish-blue morning gown. They looked as I had seen them the evening before, for the clouds high up in the sky had not dispersed, but their colour was now a pinkish golden-yellow. The sunset had made me drunk; this sunrise gave me vitality. What else could I want? I danced about in exhilaration. At last daylight flooded the scene. The Downs, in yet another garment, of dark blue satin, seemed peaceful and contented. There was no mist and the sky seemed to reach to infinity. The birds, hopping from branch to branch, sang cheerfully; and I knew that my mood of eager hope was realized.

I had promised to be back for Christmas dinner with the Keene family with whom I live, and had arranged to leave Tommy's Heath after breakfast. After saying good-bye to Tom, and wishing a merry Christmas to the rest of the house, I set off on foot for Oxford. I have often seen this city of spires and towers from the fields opposite Ripon Hall, and now I did not go by the main road but through a side-path by Youlbury Ground. First I came to Chiswell House, where the poet Robert Bridges used to live. I had recently been dipping into his poetry, and Chiswell House had a special interest for me. Though the poet is not with us in this troubled contemporary epoch, I should have liked to visit his house, but it would have disturbed the quiet of the neighbourhood if I had knocked at the door; so I took off my hat as I passed by and waved a greeting to the spiritual occupant of the house.

Presently I turned on to a path to the right along a large field. I could see in the distance a thick white vapour gathering over the valley, and enveloping everything except the prominent spire of St. Mary's Church and the unmistakable dome of the Radcliffe Camera. It was very pleasing to look down on Oxford from here, and as more towers and spires emerged I amused myself by naming them. Whether or not I gave them their right names mattered little.

I turned back. After passing a lonely building which looked like an artist's studio, I found the path descended abruptly into a thick wood. It was wet and muddy, and apparently no one had been that way before me, for there were no footmarks yet. I tried to walk noiselessly to preserve the solitude of the wood, but the birds were already singing their greeting. In case that should not be sufficient to attract my notice, they flew in and out among the branches. Near the exit from the wood, a blackbird suddenly flew down in front of me, skimmed the ground for a moment, and then rose up to a small tree in a nearby field. My eyes followed it, and I saw, beyond, a water-tower in a picturesque setting. If I had not previously seen this water-tower from Binsey Lane, I might have mistaken it for the tower of some ancient building set amid century-old tall rugged trees. I was grateful to the blackbird for directing me to this charming scene set in the clear beauty of the fields. I crossed two fields, constantly accompanied by birds fluttering about me. Perhaps they were excited at seeing the first human being that morning!

Presently I squeezed through a hedge into a newly-ploughed field, where the fresh traces of the plough formed a huge and fascinating pattern. I was full of admiration for Nature's response to man's passion for beauty. This passion is, in ordinary men, often unconscious. No doubt the ploughman had guided his plough as he had been taught to do, regardless of the pattern he was tracing in the rich brown earth. How many people refuse to realize their natural love of beauty, and are ignorant of what they themselves contribute to beauty in their daily life! How many of my fellow-artists stand aloof and think that they alone possess such high powers of imagination that they can denounce as clumsy and inartistic the common things which surround them! The beauty of the ploughed field was not in any detail, but in the entire scene. The uneven rectangle of land, the slope of the ground, the bushes, the tall trees rising here and there by the fence, and the fresh grey-brown of the soil, were all a part of the pattern. It was not like a winter scene: everything seemed so alive and vital. The birds were restive; the adjoining fields were still green, and there were many green leaves still on the bushes. The clearness and purity of the morning air enabled me to see far ahead, though the more distant trees became too small to be separated, and the colours of the hills blended with the sky. Down in the valley the many towers and spires were silhouetted still, darker now than when I saw them from the path near Chiswell House.

A flock of crows or rooks rose from the field in front of the elegantly-twisted branches of two trees outside a nearby house. They wheeled and settled again, only to fly up once more when I moved on. They entertained me with a sort of flying-dance performance, uttering their interminable "caws". As they darted backwards and forwards, the trees seemed covered by a moving veil decorated with bird-designs. Sometimes this moving veil covered the dark shadowy valley where the spires and towers of Oxford lay. Sometimes the rooks as they rose from the ground were like curls of black smoke rising from the earth—as if the earth were burning. Why should such a thought come into my mind? The rooks, I thought, must be grateful for the newly-ploughed field, so expressive of the willingness of English people to "dig for victory", to save them scraping hard to find their food.

Near the wooden gate leading to the adjoining field I met the first human being I had encountered on my walk—a white-bearded old man with a small brown dog. Two more fields and I reached the high road. Some old cottages came into sight, presumably the village of North Hinksey; then I passed the village church and stood on the weathered stone bridge. It was so quiet that I could clearly hear the organ and the Christmas morning service, and the sweet voice of the running water beneath the bridge seemed to harmonize with the deeper tones of the organ. I had never found organ music so charming and appealing before.

In the two parapets of the bridge I saw the embrasures where the warriors of old probably stood to guard their city, and my thoughts turned to the soldiers of our own day. Here, amid these historic surroundings that had witnessed battles of yore, I sent a silent greeting to the British warriors of today who have guarded this country so gallantly and enabled me to continue my Silent Travels in peace. I also sent greetings far away, to my own country, where my countrymen have stood firm for five long years, so that succeeding generations may enjoy peace in the years to come. How I long to see my land again and regret that I am not sharing with my own people the perils and the agonies of war!

I walked on between two rows of tall trees lining the road until I came to Ferry Hinksey Road. Turning to the right I came to an old smaller bridge leading to the beautiful ancient Osney Town Church. I stood for a while on the bridge listening to the shallow water running beneath, so pure and clear that I could see the small stones at the bottom. I felt a deep conviction that the turmoils of our day would pass away like the running water and none of the fanatical obsessions of expansionists and conquerors be left to muddy the pure stream of civilization.

I passed under the railway arch and went home by the canal. At the point where the water falls from the inner canal to the outer one, the loud chatter of swans fell on my ear. But there were no swans on the canal, and I discovered to my surprise that the noise came from swans on the pond in Worcester College gardens. When the trees are in leaf the pond is invisible from the canal, but now the swans could see me between the bare branches. They stretched their necks and raised their wings and gave me the full voice of their friendly greeting.

I had had the lively company of birds all the way, and their singing rang in my ears long after I had reached home.

It had been a wonderful Christmas morning.

22
A Brief Session of Painting

ONE Friday afternoon in February 1942 a friend of mine, Professor John Wheatley, the Director of the Graves Art Gallery, Sheffield, sent me a wire asking me to lunch with him in Oxford on the following Sunday. It seemed to me that as he was visiting me at Oxford I should be the host, but argument on the point would have to wait.

I had not seen Wheatley since I was in Sheffield in January 1940. We had on many occasions planned to meet again, but were always thwarted by one difficulty or another. He meanwhile had become busier and busier. Since 1940, in addition to his many jobs as Professor of Art and Director of the Art Gallery, he has held the rank of major in the Home Guard. What an interesting combination! He has a great sense of humour; no sooner was he in uniform than he wrote to me expressing the hope that I would not look down on him, for the Chinese are supposed not to rank soldiers very high in society!

He had not turned up when the clock struck two, and at two-thirty it did not seem as if he would come. But suddenly there he was outside my door, and I was very happy to see him again after so long. He explained the difficulties of the journey. The heavy snow had only just disappeared, and the bitter north wind was blowing harshly, but we tingled with the warmth of the geniality of our friendship. What a bright moment it was in these dark and tedious days of war!

We lunched at the George Restaurant in George Street by a window facing Broad Street. I have been several times to this restaurant, which in spite of wartime food restrictions still serves unexpected customers. The George, I am told, used before the war to be a meeting-place for undergraduates, who merely signed for their meals and paid the full amount at the end of term. The proprietor must have had frequent difficulty in collecting his debts, but apparently he did not mind. Probably he would not mind now; but where are the flocks of undergraduates? The number of college students has greatly diminished, for most of them were of military age and have been called up. The present students are exceptionally young and include a number of resident foreigners. The head-waiter, an old white-haired smiling man, must regret the changed atmosphere now that his restaurant is filled with uniform-wearers instead of those noisy youngsters with their political enthusiasms, but he keeps cheerful.

While we were waiting for coffee we heard a military band playing in the street below. Most of the customers came to the window to look, and we also stood up. Wheatley told me proudly that he himself had some time ago led a big company of Home Guards taking part in a Warship Week parade in Sheffield, and he admitted that the Oxford procession was a fine long one. He said with a smile that soldiers did not like marching behind sailors because of the latter's special step. Now that he was directly connected with the Home Guard he felt a personal pride in the procession.

I noticed a woman in W.R.N.S. uniform put her chin up firmly when a company of Wrens appeared in the parade. In fact, the parade was all chin-up. This chin-up business has interested me much since the war began. I have seen the expression many a time in the newspapers, but did not quite understand it until I saw Jack Hulbert at the Oxford New Theatre. I have often wondered why the phrase "chins up" should be used to encourage people to endure the difficulties of war-time. Mussolini, one feels, must be considered adept at keeping his chin up: he once looked so hard at the sky that he did not see a big stone on the unpaved Abyssinian road. Walking on the unpaved road of life with chin up is always dangerous, and gives a person a contemptuous air. I hope that ladies in particular will not try to conduct their civil life with their chins perpetually up.

We left the George to go to my rooms. The parade was still in the main street and the 'buses had stopped for the time being, so we walked through Gloucester Road and St. John's Street into Wellington Square. The yellow-black of the walls, and the arrangement of the rows of houses in St. John's Street, are perhaps typical of the Oxford licensed houses for undergraduates. The cheerful sky-gazing manner of some passing undergraduates brought back my thoughts to the phrase "chin-up". Wheatley expressed his disapproval of undergraduates generally, dubbing them a conceited lot. I replied that Oxford undergraduates were perhaps entitled to be conceited, seeing how fortunate they were in being able to study in Oxford, particularly in the present difficult circumstances.

I have always thought that the short period of one's life spent at college is the sweetest of all, and that when one leaves college one cannot help but regret—

> *That time is past,*
> *And all its aching joys are now no more,*
> *And all its dizzy raptures.*

This regret unfortunately does not necessarily mean that one has lost the conceit acquired during college days. What upsets me is that those who have learned most about life become more conceited than ever. The more one knows the more modest one should be, because there is much to know and so little worth being proud of in our scanty knowledge. I cannot understand why many elderly people talk so positively about what they know.

While we were walking past the Clarendon Press in Walton Street a story came into my mind. In a certain Chinese village there once lived a man who enjoyed telling people that he had seen a giant whose head touched the sky while his feet were still on earth. One day he met another man who said that *he* knew a giant whose upper lip touched the sky while the lower one was on the ground. The first man asked what happened to his body, and the second answered that he had only seen him with his mouth open. Wheatley laughed at my story.

No sooner had we reached my rooms than Wheatley, who for some time has been practising Chinese technique in painting, took some brushes from his breast pocket and paper from his bag, and without loss of time asked me how Chinese artists achieve a certain shade of ink-colour in a particular stroke. He admitted that he had come here both to see me and to watch how I handled the brush in making such a stroke. It was then past three-thirty, and Wheatley emphasized that he must not miss his five-o'clock train.

What strength of impulse there must have been to drive him so long a journey for so short a meeting! And what a novel experience for me after nine years in the material, practical atmosphere of England! Such an incident, of course, would not be rare in China among friends with common interests. One popular story tells how one day Huan Yi, a great musician who never failed to carry his *Ti*, a bamboo-pipe, met Wang Hui-Chih, a renowned contemporary man of letters, on the riverside at Ching-Hsi. Although they had never met before, Wang asked Huan to play his favourite pipe for him before he went any further. At that time Huan was very prosperous and held high office in the government, but he followed Wang into a wood by the side of the road and played. Afterwards they went their separate ways without exchanging a word.

I remember how when I was young friends would drop in to see my father, paint with him for a little while and then leave. Such incidents were considered to denote true culture. So I was even more thrilled at Wheatley's second motive for his visit than his first. This unexpected event breaking the monotony of my minutely-regulated life, gave me great pleasure.

We at once began to paint, each making a drawing of a bird, mine a wild duck, Wheatley's a duckling. Then we made two joint-paintings. On one Wheatley drew three bamboos and I added two little chicks, and on the other we painted a group of bamboos. It was by then time for Wheatley to go. He took three of the paintings with him and left one collaboration for me which, though accomplished in such an unusual manner, proved not a bad effort. Wheatley was gone, and we had not even exchanged the usual greetings and enquiries. Real friendship does not depend on such trifles.

The work Wheatley and I did together still hangs in my room. The more I look at it, the more attached to it I become. James Agate recently wrote an article on music called "A Mixed Bag", beginning with the words: "A friend of mine, asked what was the most remarkable thing he had seen in an adventurous life, replied, 'A man in Fleet Street consuming simultaneously oysters, porridge and cider.' I said that for a bet I would do the same with kipper, tripe and crème de menthe." I was amused but also interested in this notion, not because we Chinese have a craze for betting, as I have—incredibly—been told, but because I picture James Agate as a typical Englishman disliking anything which upsets his routine, and yet here he is prepared to do something quite absurd merely for a bet. I wonder whether he would think that Wheatley and I did our joint painting on the strength of a bet?

23
Pleasant Noises

DISTURBING thoughts had been troubling my mind all day, and I had found it impossible to concentrate on work. Was this due to the news of the recent reverses in the Far East? Hardly; for I have never had much news from my family since the invaders occupied my native city, Kiu-kiang, on 23 July, 1938, and I have had to learn not to brood. Was it due to tiredness after finishing the writing and illustrating of my first novel, *The Men of the Burma Road*? No; for I always experience joy in writing and painting what interests me, and such work seldom tires me. What, then, had been bothering me the whole day?

I sat down after supper that evening with a book of Wordsworth's poems. As I turned the pages idly my eye was caught by these lines:

It is the first mild day of March:
Each minute sweeter than before,
The red-breast sings from the tall larch
That stands beside our door.

There is a blessing in the air,
Which seems a sense of joy to yield
To the bare trees, and mountains bare,
And grass in the green field.

. . . .
. . . .

No joyless forms shall regulate
Our living calendar:
We from today, my Friend, will date
The opening of the year.

Love, now an universal birth,
From heart to heart is stealing,
From earth to man, from man to earth:
It is the hour of feeling.

One moment now may give us more
Than years of toiling reason:
Our minds shall drink at every pore
The spirit of the season.

Some silent laws our hearts will make,
Which they shall long obey:
We for the year to come may take
Our temper from today.

And from the blessed power that rolls
About, below, above,
We'll frame the measure of our souls:
They shall be tuned to love.

Then come, my Sister! come, I pray,
With speed put on your woodland dress;
And bring no book: for this one day
We'll give to idleness.

I have not yet acquired the habit of differentiating between weekdays and Sundays, nor of remembering dates precisely, so it was a surprise to me to find that it was the first day of March, 1942. I at once put on my overcoat and went out to drink the "spirit of the season".

But it was too chilly; the weather was anything but mild on this particular first day of March! It would soon be a beautiful moonlight night, but the moon was still hidden by thick clouds, so I returned home. I had seen in the *Oxford Mail* that there would be an eclipse that night.

Twilight over St. Giles

Evening view of St. Aldate's

My depression had been shaken off, and my mind was filled with the thoughts of spring so beautifully expressed by Wordsworth. I decided to spend the next day out of doors, for after fits of depression I always seek solace in the open air. For one reason or another I did not set out until half-past three the next afternoon. The 'bus conductress called out "Headington", and I found myself at the gate of Bury Knowle Park under a well-shaped pine-tree. I had not been there since I came to Oxford more than a year before, though I had passed through many a time when travelling by coach to London or Aylesbury.

The name Headington will always be associated in my mind with a friend of mine, the late A. D. Brankstone of the Old Mill, Twyford. I met Brankstone while he was assisting at the Exhibition of Chinese Art at Burlington House in 1935. He was born in China and became an ardent student of Chinese art, especially of pottery and porcelain, on which he wrote a most interesting book. In 1938 he joined the Ceramic Department of the British Museum. When war broke out he was transferred to the Far East Section of the Ministry of Information. In those early days of war he clearly foresaw that relations between England and China would become closer, and he offered to go out to China at a moment's notice on behalf of the Ministry of Information and the British Council. Shortly before leaving, Brankstone asked me to accompany him and his father to Oxford to see some friends. As we approached Headington, something went wrong with the car, and Brankstone stopped to put it right. That was my first acquaintance with Headington.

A few months later, after I had been bombed out of my London flat and had come to live in Oxford, I heard that Brankstone had fallen seriously ill on the journey to China, and had died in a Hong Kong hospital. His death was a heavy blow. I had recently had too much bad news of my own relatives and friends in China to be sentimental any longer, but I was upset that a young fellow like Brankstone should have died so suddenly. He was only just over thirty. His death was most untimely, not only because England thereby lost an expert student of Chinese art and culture, but because he had such a clear vision of the future relations between England and China, and his efforts to make my countrymen understand the English would have greatly benefited both our countries.

We had often discussed together how we could best do our bit to bring our two peoples to mutual understanding. Few English people realize the imperative need of this. It might not occur to them that a Chinese living in this country as professional man or student, could perform a double duty by smoothing out any misunderstandings about China. I often wonder whether Englishmen living in China feel it their duty to interpret their countrymen to the Chinese. Brankstone did. And whenever my thoughts return to the importance of mutual understanding between England and China, I remember Brankstone and deplore his untimely death.

Now that I was in Headington in the very beginning of March I thought of Brankstone. I stood at the gate of the park for a while reflecting that it was but a short time since he and I were there. How quickly time slips by, and how quickly changes occur! Presently I was roused by the sound of dogs barking inside the park, so I went in. Two little dogs were chasing each other, barking incessantly. One of them was a Pekingese who, having been born in England, was naturally a British subject but had retained his Chinese face and might be expected, like any true Chinese, to be ready to welcome a fellow-countryman. We were too far apart, however, and he did not notice me, but I was interested in the sound of his bark. He had certainly *not* acquired an Oxford accent, nor yet that of an evacuee from East London. It may be that to English ears it sounded as strange as Chinese—to me it sounded familiar and pleasant. How sentimental and nationalistic I seemed to be at that moment!

No sooner had the barking faded in the distance than a flock of rooks began to caw. I do not know whether there are any rooks in China, but I remember in my younger days that the older members of my family did not care for the noise of crows. When I grew up I came across many beautiful phrases about crows in T'ang poems, and noticed that crows played an important part in paintings by Sung and Yuan masters. This is because these birds, with their black bodies, seem, as they return to their rookery on winter evenings, or perch in ones and twos on the top branches of a tall bare tree, to symbolize the spirit of winter. They are impressive and decorative in their aloofness. I like to put them in my own paintings, because our ink-and-wash is an extremely good medium for them. I have never wholly recovered from my objection to their cawing—probably a prejudice remaining from my youth—but rooks, possibly merely because they had a different name, did not irritate me at all. The rooks

With noisy caw
Are foraging for sticks and straw,

as an English poet, maybe Mary Howitt, has written. Their black bodies stood out against the spacious green of the small park, and they seemed to enjoy being conspicuous on the lower branches of the trees round the outskirts of the grounds. Wordsworth was right to say:

There is a blessing in the air
Which seems a sense of joy to yield
To the bare trees....

The noisy caw was the blessing today! The scene before me was a perfect early Yuan picture, perhaps even a late Sung one, and I was altogether absorbed. Then I remembered a story about rooks which I had recently read in an old English book:

There was once in a rookery a pair of birds, who, in the building time, instead of going out in search of materials, kept at home, and watching the opportunity, plundered every unguarded nest, thus building their own habitation by contributions levied upon the industry of their neighbours. This had continued some time, and the robbers had hitherto escaped with impunity; their nest was just finished, when the rest of the society, by common consent, made an attack on the depredators, beat them soundly, demolished their nest, and expelled them ignominiously from the rookery.

The perfect counterpart to the aggressors and invaders of the whole world today. I pray that the allied nations may soon expel them ignominiously from the community of decent men. Unfortunately men are more astute than rooks, and find it more difficult to make a simple decision and carry out a plan by common consent!

My thoughts were becoming involved, and as I have always tried not to mix nature and politics, I left the Park. I had wanted to see Headington again, and to go into Oxford by that route, but had not expected to find myself in Headington Park.

After strolling down the main street I wandered slowly towards Oxford. As I approached Valentia Road I saw a pleasant red-brick building in large grounds. I had already had a glimpse of its small tower between the branches of a huge tree from beyond Valentia Road, but had never before seen the whole building. It was neat and dignified, and conspicuous against its background, and I imagined it must be an educational centre since it seemed an unlikely place for a government office. I wondered whether in two or three hundred years' time visitors to Oxford would include this mellowed building in their sightseeing. I liked the atmosphere of spacious dignity so well that I crossed the road to look more closely. At that moment a crowd of girl students streamed out, checking their rush to stare happily at me. Some stopped talking suddenly, some smiled, and others started to chatter again with even more liveliness. No doubt many were interested in my flat face! I was attracted by the cheerful babel of voices, though I could not catch a single word.

The name "Gipsy Lane" nearby suggested something unusual and mysterious. The lane wound away from me into a cloud of mist, yet I knew that if I walked into it I should find no mist. I wonder why this lane is called "Gipsy"? Most probably it has nothing to do with gipsies. As I knew no way of finding out the answer to this interesting point, I moved on.

My walk was no great distance, yet by the time I reached Magdalen Bridge I was dawdling and my legs felt like lead. I crossed the Bridge and was refreshed on seeing the beautiful tracery of the leafless branches, and the bold trunks of the trees. I walked more slowly than ever, but no longer through weariness. In order to have a good look at the many lovely trees in the grounds of Magdalen School, I sat down on a public seat directly opposite some majestic poplars. I have only become acquainted with poplars since I came to England. We Chinese have always loved looking at the gnarled and crooked old trees so abundant in China, which have been praised many times for their strength and artistic shape by our poets and painters. We have a term for them, "P'an lung", which compares them to a celestial dragon coiling itself spirally. We also like trees such as the Shan, a kind of fir, and thick tall bamboos which grow straight to great heights, but I find that the little branches round the big trunks of the poplar make it more interesting than either the Shan or the bamboo. It suggests to me a grandparent surrounded by generations of descendants, in a harmonious family life. It gives a feeling of uprightness. A mysterious hand seemed to drag me from my seat to stand before these people, and I wondered if they had this strange hypnotic power on people who live their lives in their own unorthodox way. They were the dominating feature of the gardens, round which pivoted many smaller lives.

I crossed the road to look at that soaring giant, Magdalen Tower; I knew that the Tower was probably built before the poplars were planted, but I preferred to think that its architecture was planned to harmonize with the tall clean lines of the poplars. I learn from them all I need to know of straight and true conduct in life, and feel that I have no need of lessons from professors.

Just then, as though in approval of my philosophy, the pleasant voices of a flock of homing rooks and other birds greeted me, and I was reminded of my walk in Bury Knowle Park. The birds dived like swift arrows or chattered incessantly in the tree-tops, Magdalen Tower standing always soaring in the background. The blue-grey of the sky blended with the purplish-grey of the tower, yet each had its own distinctiveness. The evening mist softened the dark colour of the birds and blurred the black branches and trunks of the trees so that they looked paler and were less strongly contrasted with the other shades of colour. Everywhere was a blurred softness, like a dream.

I wanted to see the Tower at evening, so I walked along to Rose Lane near the Botanic Garden building. The birds fluttering round the tree-tops were no longer to be seen, but their pleasant noise seemed to have grown so loud that the noise of the traffic was scarcely audible. The evening light shone on the college wall and the Tower stood out clearly through the black trees. Another picture for me to paint!

Warm and snug before the fire after my walk, I felt grateful to Wordsworth for his spiritual assistance, and took down the volume of his poems again.

24
The Northern Breeze

IT must have been the northern breeze, for I could feel it coming from the direction of the tall trees behind the college barges while I was walking along the tow-path from Folly Bridge. It was a chilly morning in the middle of March, and there had evidently been a heavy frost the previous night. But I felt refreshed and different from what I felt about the boisterous so-called "March" winds of a few days before. It told me in a low voice, as it playfully wrinkled the surface of the Isis, that spring was on the way. I searched for her footsteps in the bleak countryside, finding them at last among the brightening green of the grass by the roadside, and among the branches of the trees which seemed to exude through their nakedness a purplish-green vapour. Two swans floated briskly down the stream, and the song of the blackbird and thrush could be heard. I strolled on in complete solitude, for it was evidently too early in the year for the city dwellers, who prefer to wait until spring is well on the way before venturing out into the country. They do not seem to realize that her life is very brief, and that no other delight can equal the first glimpse of her.

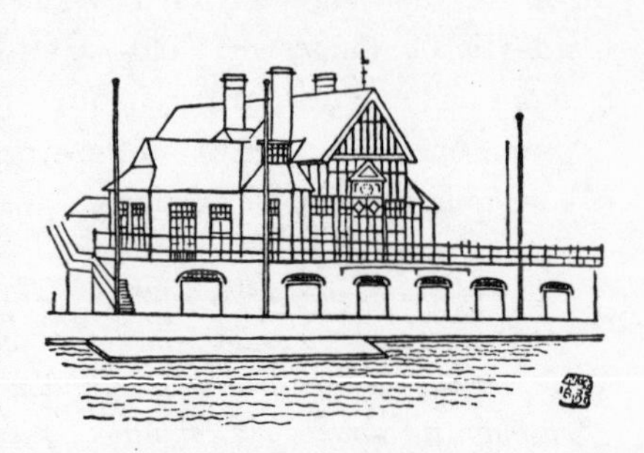

University boathouse

I passed the University boathouse, where, only two days ago, I had watched the last of the Oxford Torpids of 1942. I recalled that evening. At about five-thirty the chosen crews arrived for the race. I knew nothing of the procedure: I could not even distinguish the boat of one college from that of another; but the cheerful faces were good to see. Owing to the war there were very few spectators.

A Blue

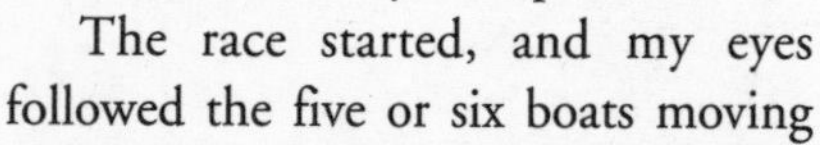

The race started, and my eyes followed the five or six boats moving rapidly down the river. The watching undergraduates shouted excitedly, though not, it seemed to me, with the same wild enthusiasm as on the occasion when I saw the race in London. I expect Oxford people are used to boat races; or perhaps the evacuees to Oxford are not accustomed to Oxford traditions. I wished I were an undergraduate to appreciate their jokes, for they were in high spirits.

Yet I was puzzled. I have been told that Oxford policemen are specially trained to deal with uncontrollable groups of undergraduates during the Torpids, the Eights, and the Oxford and Cambridge boat race. It used to be a common occurrence, I have also been told, for shop windows to be broken by intoxicated young men, or for the dome of the Radcliffe Camera to be painted red. But this crowd of students beside me showed no sign of any such irregularities, and many people say that Oxford is no longer the "old Oxford". I wonder whether the old clamour will ever be heard again after the war?

Some one has written about the general effect on the undergraduates of rowing in the Torpids or Eights:

> *...A means of social intercourse which often enables men of different taste to see and rub against each other, and also tends to make the college as a whole identify itself with its rowing representatives... Snobbishness cannot live under such conditions; jealousy can have no place in the presence of rivalry; and egotism, whether intellectual, moral, or social,*

must gradually give way before the genial warmth and physical energy of training. Thus men who row together come to be tolerant. They come to realize that there are other types, other aspirations, and other modes of thought than their own, and so they learn the great lesson which life at Oxford teaches, for the most part unconsciously, but none the less most thoroughly, to tolerate others and take them as you find them.

I had no idea that rowing had such a good influence on undergraduates! And I wondered when reading this passage whether such pursuits should not be introduced into Chinese universities on this account. Surely the fact of having been members of the same crew does not seriously influence their differences of opinion on politics and other subjects? Anyhow, rowing is certainly good exercise... And, equally certainly, I have wandered too far from my subject.

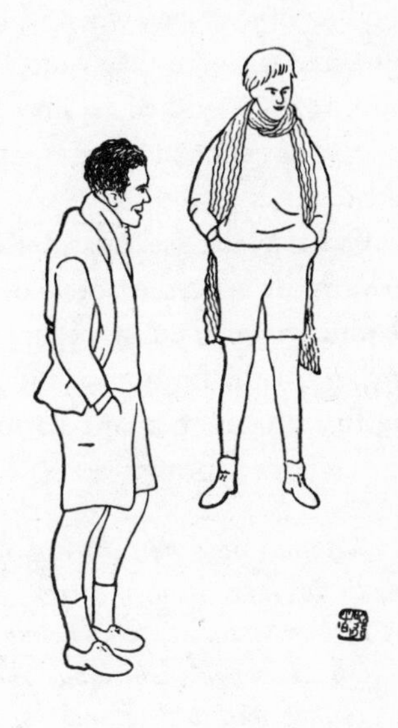

Two Blues

I had a good view of the race. Two boats were practically level, and seemed in the distance to be motionless. As the evening closed in the river-banks grew shadowy, and the river seemed to blend with the sky. The boats, floating on and on in this vast sky, were distinguished only by the white shirts of their crews. I was so enthralled by the beautiful scene that I did not realize I had moved so near to the edge of the water until I heard the shouts of those spectators on their bicycles.

Presently I reached the Free Ferry Footbridge, a huge arch bestriding a tiny stream of the Isis, and commanding the landscape. I have never before seen a bridge so dominate its surroundings, not even the huge bridges of China, Switzerland, and France, where rocky hills and great stretches of water add to their magnitude. Even Waterloo Bridge in

London cannot isolate itself from the closely-packed buildings along the river-banks. The Free Ferry footbridge seemed, with its overpowering personality, almost too vast. It dwarfed the Isis beneath, and the little boats bobbing up and down, and the scattered boathouses and cottages and trees on the shore. The designer of the bridge had doubtless good reason for having so huge an arch. He may have had in mind the flooding of the river, when its bed would become wider, or he may have visualized the grand view of Oxford from such an erection. I personally think that he wished to impress Nature with this triumph of human endeavour, not knowing that Nature would not countenance such audacity.

Close to the Isis boathouse I noticed a small stone monument in memory of a devotee of Oxford rowing. It made me think that this Oxford oarsman must occupy a great place in the history of Oxford rowing. At the bottom of the monument I saw the tiny yellow bud of the first crocus. Bernard Barton has well described the finding of the first crocus of spring:

Welcome, mild harbinger of Spring,
To this small nook of earth;
Feeling and fancy fondly cling
Round thoughts which owe their birth
To thee, and to the humble spot
Where chance has fix'd thy lowly lot.

. . . .

Yet not the lily, nor the rose,
Though fairer far they be,
Can more delightful thoughts derive
Than I derive from thee:
The eye their beauty may prefer;
The heart is thy interpreter!

This tiny speck of yellow cheered me considerably. I became very fond of the crocus when I had been in England for a time, and now understand why English people have so strong an attachment to it, for it brings them the first news of spring after the *long* English winter.

During my first two years in this country my mind was full of many things seen and heard in a strange land, and the long winters passed unnoticed. In spite of this I cannot resist claiming that I do now know something of damp and dreary English winters, though perhaps I do not find them quite so dreary as the English people, for I love the countryside at this season—snow, the beautiful lines of the naked trees, and the morning fog. But my joy at seeing the first crocus is no less heartfelt than that of the Englishman; indeed, I might be considered to have now acquired the English habit in this respect.

This first crocus on that March morning brought other thoughts to my mind besides Bernard Barton's poem. It reminded me that spring had come again and I was still in England. England has now become my second home, but I long to return soon to my own country. As though perceiving my sadness, the crocus seemed to half-open its eye and smile at me as much as to say that it enjoyed seeing me here again this spring.

The word crocus is very old and probably originated from the Greek, but I cannot remember having seen this flower grow in China. The crocus is a herald of spring in England, but in China the winter-plum blooms in the thick snows of January or February. The winter plum is a flowering tree, and that is perhaps why we Chinese prefer flowering trees to herbaceous flowers. English people seem to be more attached to the latter. For me I have now grown very fond of both of them.

I continued on my way and passed a number of golden crocuses in the front gardens of Isis Cottage, next to the Isis boathouse, and the Isis Hotel. Roughly engraved on the surface of a small and weathered antique stone bridge were names, now almost unrecognizable, of unknown visitors. How typical, I thought, of the human craving for fame! This part of the river Isis is very beautiful. I stood on the bridge. Beneath in the green meadow on the opposite bank brown-and-white cows lay lazily chewing the cud. The northern breeze had dispersed the morning mist, and the scattered red roofs of houses made bright splashes of colour.

I could hear the roar of water rushing through the weir. I love listening to running water, and even though this was not a natural waterfall it gave me pleasure. By the weir a man in uniform, probably the weir-keeper, was absorbed in fishing. I doubted whether the fish would come so near to rushing water, but the fisherman looked quite happy, evidently finding joy in the tranquillity of his pursuit rather than in the actual catching of fish. I looked back at the winding tow-path I had come by. The yellow-brown ribbon of the tow-path and the silvery streak of the river seemed to merge finally and irrevocably in a misty unity.

A mare and her foal were happily chasing each other among a group of horses. A man with a length of rope appeared, and after great difficulty succeeded in putting a noose round the neck of a big white horse and in leading it away. The horse, rebellious at first, at length became quiet, evidently realizing that work had to be done. The foal trotted to the wooden gate through which the man and horse had passed, and stared in wonder. The mare joined it, and the foal, rubbing its head on its mother's neck, seemed to ask why the horse had been taken away and where it had gone. The mother tried to drag the young one away from the gate as if to stem its curiosity about the future. Doubtless they took the future more as a matter of course than we humans do, but I, who unfortunately possess the attribute of self-consciousness, begin to wonder myself about what will happen to them.

I have always admired the patience and obedience of milk-cart horses, and I remember once seeing one which had been told to stand near the post office in St. Aldate's Street. An old man tried to stroke the horse's neck while at the same time talking to a friend. Then he turned to caress its face, but the horse did not seem to like it, and moved its head trying to avoid being made a fuss of, at the same time obviously not wishing to annoy the man. This was no life for a horse (if it can be said that horses have a life of their own). Richard Jefferies, in his *The Story of My Heart*, wrote

> *They* [dogs and horses] *are useful to us, they show more or less sympathy with us, they possess, especially the horse, a certain grace of movement. A gloss, as it were, is thrown over them by these attributes and by familiarity. The shape of the horse to the eye has become conventional: it is accepted. Yet the horse is not in any sense human. Could we look at it suddenly, without previous acquaintance, as at strange fishes in a tank, the ultra-human character of the horse would be apparent. It is the*

curves of the neck and body that carry the horse without adverse comment. Examine the hind legs in detail, and the curious backward motion, the shape and anti-human curves become apparent.

This describes well the difference in thought regarding the relations between animals and human beings. People appear to think that a horse must be made to behave like a human being. This seems selfish to me. Why can a horse not live like a horse?

I had come near to the beautiful grey Iffley Church, said to be one of the oldest churches in Oxford and the most artistically decorated inside. I had often meant to visit this church, but so far had not because I prefer to imagine those beauties so well described in guide-books. This church, standing on a high bank half hidden by trees, reminded me of the roof of an ancient monastery glimpsed through the tree-tops in some great Chinese masterpiece.

I went on until I saw a train approaching the railway bridge with a clatter. The tranquillity of the scene was at once dissipated, and I turned back home. Nothing hindered my steps, yet I felt that the northern breeze was trying to stop me and keep me a little longer. It was this northern breeze which had given life to the flowers and trees by the river, though they still wore their shabby winter clothes. It is this invisible life in the steadily-running water, the fresh soil, the mossy banks, the cold balmy air and the chattering notes of the birds, which tempts me to walk by the Isis at this time of year.

Passing over Folly Bridge I recalled what I had seen while walking there in the autumn with a friend. Two swans, one old and one nearly grown, were floating against a tide running strongly from where the Isis joins the Thames. The old swan was an expert at floating, moving its two big feet-flappers together so that its body was pushed some distance at each stroke. It made a pretty show. When confronted by the tumbling water where the rivers join, it turned back, and showed clearly that it did not want to move any farther. The young one flapped its feet one at a time—a very strenuous effort—but the rapidly-moving water pushed it back. The cygnet was not discouraged and struggled on, sometimes quacking with disappointment. My eyes followed it until it reached the other side. I was pleased to see it win that hard struggle and float peacefully along as if nothing had happened. It might, when it stretched its long neck, appear proud of itself; but that was certainly not because its fellow-swans had praised it, as human beings would have done to one of their fellows.

I thought of the old swan which had given up the struggle, knowing that there was nothing to be gained in the end on the other side of the bridge. I also thought of the young one, full of the spirit of adventure, and determined to will through whether for gain or not. In these fateful days in the history of the world I would rather retain the adventurous spirit of the young swan than take the line of least resistance of the old one, no matter how reasonable its arguments. My friend, with a smile, had agreed.

Iffley Church

Above the distant trees a host of rooks gossip in the sunset;
The little bridge and the running water are like those in my homeland.
The chimes of the bells vibrate in pursuit of the rising mist,
In the midst of the emerald green lies the ancient church.

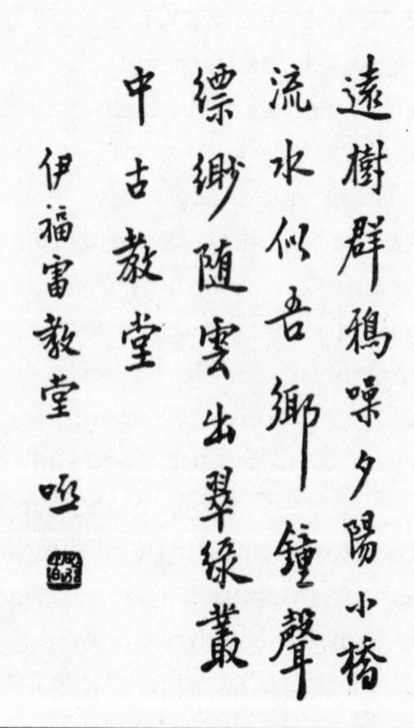

25
Cold, Yet not Cold

DOUBLE Summer Time began in 1942 on April. April days in England cannot usually be called warm, and I am therefore the more struck by the infinite purposefulness of the English mind which, in its desire to control things, excludes nothing, not even Time, which we Chinese regard as so immutable. It is useless to ask whether English people would not rather breakfast at six o'clock instead of eight o'clock, thus making use of the early daylight; their inborn conservatism would be greatly shocked should breakfast be served at any other time than eight. Theoretically I do not think the English are a very practical or realistic people, although they have a gift for suiting everything to their own purposes. Any Chinese, a poet in particular, would be amused at the idea of the summer sun setting at nine o'clock instead of seven. After a few years' stay in this country, however, I have grown used to daylight at "ten o'clock" at night.

After seeing the ballet at the New Theatre one night I found it was daylight outside. The air was fresh, and my mind cleared after the warm atmosphere. It seemed too early to go home. I jostled my way quickly through the crowd to the equally crowded Cornmarket Street, but as I crossed Carfax into St. Aldate's Street the crowd thinned, although I could hear behind me snatches of discussion about the dancers. An almost full moon was high in the sky, and I noticed how clear was Tom Tower of Christ Church while the opposite buildings seemed unusually dark.

In my delight I was torn between an impulse to proceed to Folly Bridge and one to go through the Memorial Gate to stroll among the lofty trees of the Broad Walk. Eventually I found myself walking down the High towards Magdalen Bridge. The moon was now risen and lit up the street like daylight. The magnificent spire of St. Mary's Church dominated all else, and the top of Queen's College gateway was sharp and clear. Oxford 'buses do not run now after half-past nine, and it gave me a chilly feeling to see the street so empty of traffic. The intense quiet of the High was heightened by the clear echo of the footsteps of an occasional passer-by, and I remembered a quotation from a great Chinese poet written one summer day: "The wood grows quieter while the cicada whirls on and on with its noisy cry."

Gateway of Queen's

On Magdalen Bridge I leaned against the low wall and found myself gazing at the moon in the shining mirrored surface of the Cherwell. A soft haze settled round the trunks of the trees in front of Magdalen School and the Botanic Garden, muffling the silence. The birds, I thought, must be sleeping, and the fish resting motionless on the river-bed. I could imagine the birds asleep, their tiny eyes shut and their heads beneath their wings, but how, I wondered, do fishes sleep? Do they just lie still in the water? Or perhaps they do not rest at all? I have never seen a fish with its eyes shut. No doubt the scientists have their theories. I did not really expect my question to be answered, and to tell the truth, I was not interested. Let it remain a mystery to me. Mystery stirs the imagination, and the tranquillity of this moonlight night through it grew more intense in contrast to my mind's activities. Longfellow's lines found an answering chord in my heart:

Then the moon in all her pride,
Like a spirit glorified,
Filled and overflowed the night
With revelations of her light.

The pond, University Park

Summer along the Cherwell

And the poet's song again,
Passed like music through my brain;
Night interpreted to me
All its grace and mystery.

Although the river was scarcely visible there, from somewhere behind a tiny bush near the dark veil of trees I could see the stern of a rowing-boat or punt, motionless on the dreaming water. It was April and spring was only just awake. The young leaves above my head were so scattered that I could count them, and the moonlight tinted them an unreal shade of green. How different colours are in the light of sun and moon! The sun gives warm, lively tints of yellow and red, while the grey-blue tints of the moon give peace and calm to the troubled heart.

My delight at seeing the rich gold of daffodils by the greenhouse in the Botanic Garden was perhaps enhanced by my fancy that they were a group of dainty fairies dancing in yellow robes. Before them, on the dark carpet of the river-bank, hundreds of tiny white daisy-fairies kept time in the dance, which caused a soft breeze to blow graciously on my face and brought back to mind the ballet I had watched a few hours before. The human ballet had stirred, while the floral ballet subdued, my emotions.

The wind was rising, and the moon shifted restlessly in the quivering water, whose ripples chased each other in carefree delight. But where did the first ripple go, and where did the last come from? Another mystery. The power of the water could bend the moon's reflection into many curves, but it could never break her to pieces, and at times she resumed her round smoothness. I saw her first as a piece of the purest white jade of a T'ang disc of the seventh century AD; then when I saw on her face a dark shadow, as the archaic jade of a Chou or Han disc of two or three thousand years ago, marked by the shadow of age. I wonder if the moon has changed since she first existed? A T'ang poet, Chang Jo-Shu, once wrote:

Who first looked at the moon along the bank of the river,
When the river moon first shone on man?
Life has no end; it goes on generation after generation;
But the river moon never changes.

Li P'o, the greatest Chinese poet of all time, has expressed the same idea:

How often is there a moon in the blue sky?
I hold up my wine-cup and ask.
Man cannot climb up to the moon,
Yet the moon follows man in his wanderings.

Modern man has not seen the ancient moon,
But the present moon shone long ago on ancient man.
Men of ancient and modern times are like running water;
But they look in the same way at the bright moon.
I only wish, at times of singing and drinking,
That the moon be often reflected in my golden wine-cup!

I thought how this same love of the moon was shared by many past generations, and would be shared by generations to come, for I cannot believe there will ever be a time when man will cease to love the moon.

Li P'o, who lived over a thousand years ago, once lifted his wine-cup to the moon in an invitation to drink with him; and from the poem I have just quoted he must have found delight in catching her in his wine-cup. He calls her his playmate; but he was not the first to think of her as a companion, for she was kept as a "pet" by a Han emperor of the first century BC! The story runs that Han Wu-ti ordered a beautiful pavilion to be built with a great lake at the foot of it in which to keep the moon for his play. He called the pavilion "Fu-Yueh-Lou" (Stooping-to-the-Moon Pavilion), or "Tiao-Yueh-Lou" (Fishing-the-Moon Pavilion), because he sometimes stooped to talk to her, like some stout Englishman bending to talk to his terrier or dachshund. Sometimes he would dangle a long fishing-rod into the lake in the hope of catching her. Sometimes he would row on the lake with the ladies of his court and play with the moon by splashing the water to ruffle her smoothness. Since then Chinese gardens have always had a lake or pond where the moon is "kept as a pet".

It is interesting, is it not, that many Chinese prefer the moon as a pet to a dog or cat. What an unpractical people we must be in English eyes, although perhaps we are practical in our own way, for we find no difficulty in feeding our pets even in wartime! But are we not, in our efforts to "pet" the moon, as determined to control nature as the English are in trying to control time?

A sudden breath of cold broke my train of thought. The clatter of footsteps on the pavement had ceased, and I felt chilly, though my heart was still full of the warmth of my thoughts. As I turned to leave the bridge I saw Magdalen Tower standing, lordly and solitary, its stone washed white by the clear moonlight. I think it is a good thing that the tower is not close to St. Mary's Spire, for otherwise they might fight to dominate the High!

I crossed to Longwall Street, a little side-road leading off the High. It was the first time I had walked there at night, though I knew it by day. There were no cars now parked by the wall. It was very empty and silent: I seemed to be the only living creature there. I strolled along, completely relaxed, with my hands clasped behind my back, as I used to walk in my native city. I felt that this corner of the world belonged to me, and at the same time that a part of me was in another world; yet it was not another world, but a familiar old world. On the shadowed side of the street the houses might have been Chinese, while the long moonlit wall round the deer park of Magdalen College exactly resembled the city wall of my birthplace, and I could imagine I was walking there. The development of the human mind the world over differs only in degree, not in essence. How is it that the English should have built a city wall similar in almost all respects to a Chinese wall, save that it consists of carefully-cut stones instead of large bricks?

In Holywell Road, where I now found myself, are some of the most typical of Oxford's old residential houses. Their owners have evidently not wished to preserve their antiquity, for some have their doors and windows painted in bright colours, even yellow. This seems very un-English. From the corner of Balliol College and St. Giles' I had the unusual view, never seen in daylight, of both the Martyrs' Memorial and the Taylorian Buildings. During the day St. Giles' is always crowded with people and traffic, and many lovers of the ancient city sigh regretfully and complain that Oxford is not at all what it used to be. This is true at first glance, but after a little time one realizes that in many ways it is the same old Oxford, particularly as the recent petrol restrictions have reduced the number of private cars. As I stood looking at the Martyrs' Memorial there was not even a military lorry in sight. The street was clear and spacious and I walked slowly down it.

A gentle breeze whispered in the trees in the middle of the street, intensifying the silence and the brightness of the moon. A few people—some old, from the sound of their footsteps, some in twos—wandered along the pavements. Their faces and dress were indistinguishable, and they might have been inhabitants of the Oxford of a hundred years ago. Was not this, I wondered, the real old Oxford after all? On the way home I composed a short poem:

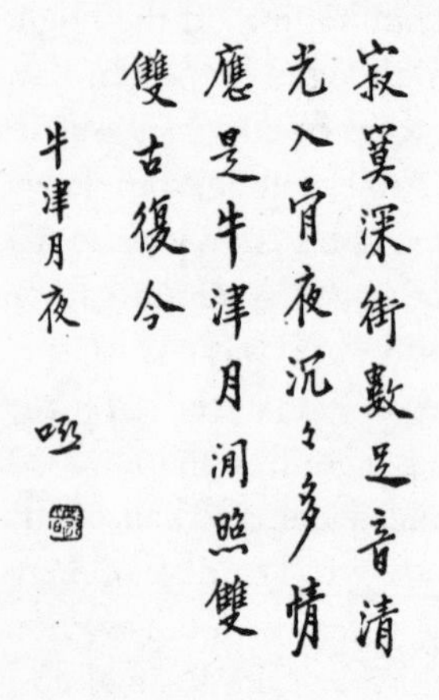

Counting the footsteps in the quiet street,
I feel the clear light penetrating and the
dead night sinking.
How sympathetic and kind the Oxford
moon must be,
Shining idly on companions walking
together
As she has done through the ages.

I was glad to have strolled so late beneath the moon, and was grateful that the curfew had been abolished for me now that China has, after five years of fighting, become an official ally. I must say I sympathized at the beginning of the war with the authorities who felt obliged to impose a curfew; but although my mind and spirit have always been free, the freedom to indulge again in silent wandering is pleasant.

So I pay homage to the moon, whose charm and brilliance induced me to wander by night and made me realize the value of absolute freedom.

The grey-blue light seemed to add coldness to the chilly April night: but it was not cold to me, for I had the warmth of a free mind. But oh, what agony to think of those trapped or enslaved in the war-shattered or occupied areas beneath the self-same moonlight!

When I got home everybody was sound asleep, so I went noiselessly and contentedly to bed.

26
Medium of Friendship

MANY of the valued friendships I enjoy in this country have arisen, neither socially nor even by introduction, but by mutual love of flowers. This passion is no respecter of persons or creeds. Like death, it is a leveller. It abolishes the boundaries of nations; it ignores the rigid dogmas that divide men; and it may well help to promote understanding in fields far outside the walls of gardens.

Many of the best-loved of English flowers are closely connected with my own country. Four or five years ago I went to Dublin on a visit to Lord and Lady Longford, both Oxford graduates. We have kept up a correspondence ever since, and as spring comes round each year they write that the fresh-blooming rhododendrons remind them of me. How charming that is!

There are, of course, many varieties of rhododendron, some hailing from the Alps, some from America; but the massive dark red variety with the big funnel-shaped flowers, and one of the pink varieties, both of which grow in China, are, I think, the ones which appeal most to English people, for they are to be found in abundance in the gardens and parks of the British Isles. I do not know when they were introduced here, nor from what country the first plants were brought, but they certainly thrive in English soil and climate. We ourselves are apt to take them for granted, for they grow wild among our hills and rocks and are to be found in many provinces in spring. The large pink variety seems to thrive particularly in central China, where it is often planted round

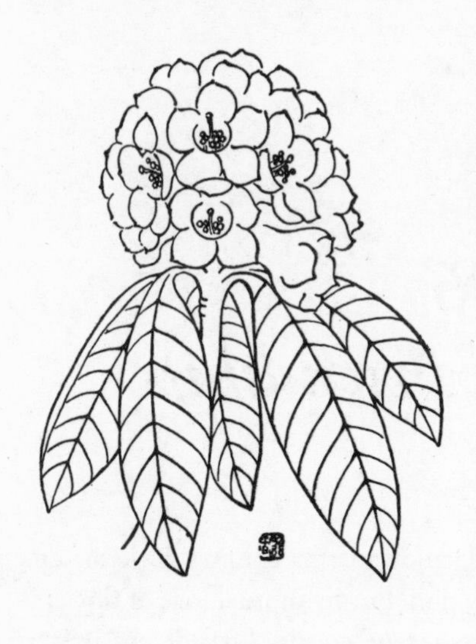

Rhododendron

ancestral tombs; and at the Ch'ing-Ming Festival, when thousands of people flock to the tombs, there is a brilliant blaze of pink. The dark red rhododendron, on the other hand, grows in great masses on the hills and mountains of south-west China. Neither variety appears to flourish in the north. The Chinese people on the whole echo the preferences in flowers of their great poets, and as few poets have immortalized the rhododendron, so the public shows little interest in it. Personally I have loved these flowers from childhood, and I am glad to see them admired outside my own country.

I am particularly grateful to them for bringing me to closer acquaintance with Lord and Lady Longford. I recently had a letter from Lady Longford in which she told me something of her life in Oxford when she was a student there:

I know I enjoyed being at college, though I complained a lot at the time, as one always complains when one is just growing up. It was pleasant to have comparative freedom, after being at school. I had a little room of my own (women in college have one room, men have two), and could stay up and talk all night to my friends and could read what books I liked, and did not have to go to lectures if I did not want to. Of course I wanted still more freedom than I had: I did not like being locked in at a certain hour; I wanted to read books quite unconnected with my studies; I did not like all the women students and professors in the college, and there were rules against seeing the men students! Those rules are mostly changed now, and anyway we broke them easily. I liked the country around Oxford and went for long walks and boating on the river, and made some friends; and there was plenty of leisure, and no trouble about housekeeping. My tutors were quite kind, and I enjoyed studying Greek and Roman literature and philosophy and history. You will have discovered that there are some learned professors in Oxford… I always preferred the ones who were old, and not at all interested in modern life, and not tidily dressed or even very clean! In those days, nobody was much interested in politics. I believe it has changed since; the students were more interested in literature and art, and we had little magazines which were very ambitious, and almost everybody tried to write poetry and short stories. We were also fond of the theatre, and there was a lot of amateur acting, which I'm afraid was very bad. Just occasionally, when there were examinations, we became terrified and worked all night; but we spent most of our time talking, and drinking tea and coffee. It was pleasant to meet foreign students, and there was a Chinese girl in my college who was much more amusing and clever than anyone. We decorated our rooms according to our own taste: I had some reproductions of French impressionist pictures, an imitation of a Byzantine ikon painted by a student of history, a Buddha, an Indian table-cloth, a plaster head of Alexander the Great which was much too big for the room, and as many brightly coloured cushions as I could collect, and a Persian rug. And we smoked Turkish and Russian and Egyptian cigarettes—which I don't like any more—and were not at all interested in food—which I am now…

It was a long letter which I much enjoyed reading for the vivid picture it gave of the life of a student a few years ago. People tell me that life at Oxford is much changed in recent years. This I cannot judge: after two years here I can only say that the Oxford professors I have met have been fashionably and neatly dressed. In my own College days I recollect one or two learned old professors of philosophy and literature, greatly respected, who were attired shabbily and untidily. I had little to do with them, being at that time busy with test-tubes and chemical bottles in the laboratory, in the fond hope of becoming a scientist. And what am I now? After re-reading Lady Longford's letter I feel ashamed to have led such an uninteresting life at College, and in future, when I see rhododendrons in bloom, I shall remember the Longfords and this picture of Oxford life.

Another friend of mine, Sir William Milner, never fails to comment each year on the blooming of the masses of spotted tiger-lilies in his rock garden, usually urging me to come and see them for myself. I share his love for tiger-lilies, as well as for many other flowers, and like to stay with him when they are in bloom. He takes me round to the back of Parcevall Hall and we stand gazing in silence before the groups of lilies. He is in the habit, when showing visitors round his garden, of explaining all the time, moving from plant to plant; but he seldom speaks to me when we are standing admiring the lilies. His face is lit with a smile of pride, and I smile too. I cannot help smiling, because each of the spotted tiger-lilies is not only smiling but roaring with laughter, especially when a gentle wind blows them and they toss their heads as if they were taking drinks in the gay bar of some luxury hotel in Piccadilly. In China we consider that flowers have a feminine character, elegant and charming, so we choose them to symbolize young ladies. Somehow I feel that this spotted lily has a masculine character; the more so when I see tall young English Captains in their elegant uniforms laughing over their drinks. Each petal of this particular lily turns back a little like a wide-open mouth. It is perhaps its lack of feminine grace which has prevented our great poets from writing verses about it. But I have heard that the Emperor Chien Lung was fond of the tiger-lily and many times ordered the Italian artist at his court, Castiglione, to paint this flower. I have seen one reproduction of his work.

Tiger-lily

B. Maund wrote in 1825:

We know of very few plants that excited more general interest than did the Tiger Lily on its introduction to this country. Every one heard of,

> *admired, and resolved on possessing, this Chinese beauty; and in a very short time, from its facility of propagation, the cottager and nobleman boasted alike of its splendour in their borders. Happily, our nature will not admit the continued exertion of these strong feelings of delight, which are generated by novelty; or, we should be unceasingly carried about by ecstasies, and temperate reason could no where build her throne.*

For me it is interesting to hear that among English people strong feelings of delight had to be controlled. The Tiger Lily was introduced into the British Isles in 1804. There are many species of lilies in China, where we call the lily *Pai-ho*, meaning "hundred-fit" or fit for a hundred purposes, signifying that it will grow in any conditions. Even the English weather suits it!

Writing about lilies brings to my mind a story about a white lily. In the tenth century a lonely traveller insisted on taking shelter in an empty, haunted temple called Kuang-hwa on the Tsu-lai mountain in Yen-chow-fu of Shangtung Province. Though he stayed on day after day, week after week, nothing happened to him. But one summer afternoon while he was gazing at the frescoes on the temple walls, suddenly a very beautiful young girl in white, about sixteen years of age, appeared coming down the long corridor. He asked her where she had come from, and the girl smilingly answered that she lived not very far from the mountain. The traveller, who knew the neighbourhood well, was positive that he had never seen any house near by, but he was attracted by the girl's beauty and pleased to see some one for a change, so he began to talk to her in a friendly way and tried to keep her with him. When he could persuade her to stay no longer, he gave her a pure white jade ring and offered to escort her home. The girl said that her parents might come to meet her and that he must not accompany her; so, sadly shutting the gate behind her, the traveller climbed up the stairs of the temple in order to observe and note carefully which direction she took. But after a hundred paces or so he lost sight of her. Leaving the temple he followed the path she had taken. It crossed a wide stretch of ground on which every shrub and plant was plainly visible. There was no trace of the girl. Darkness fell, and feeling tired he turned back. On his way he noticed in the grass an unusually fine white lily and stopped to dig it up by the roots so that he could examine it at home and see whether it was indeed a new variety. To his great surprise he found inside the bulb his pure white jade ring, and at once realized that the girl he had met was not a real person but the spirit of this lily flower. He bitterly regretted having brought the lily home, for now he would never see the beautiful girl again. After a few days he died of sorrow.

In old China it was the common belief that everything on earth is animated by a spirit which, after hundreds of years, can transform itself into a human body and soul and which may do good or harm to real human beings. Our books are full of such stories as the one I have just told, stories which must, I think, have been written by lonely scholars deprived by the sophisticated Confucian thought of the opportunity of meeting young girls. It is to be hoped that my story will not lead some English lad to seek adventure by living in disused temples or haunted places. Beware, young English girls, of planting the Tiger Lily in your garden lest its spirit transform itself into a tall young captain!

So far I have heard nothing strange about the lilies in my friend's garden, and perhaps I had better not say any more about flower spirits lest no more Chinese flowers be planted in this country and I lose one way of getting friends. But I will confess that though I have seen no spotted tiger lilies in Oxford, there must be plenty, for I have seen so many tall young captains!

William is a true Oxford man. When I wrote to him about the heavy snowfall in January 1941—

> *"Yes," he answered, "I can imagine your delight in wandering round Oxford in the snow; though I shouldn't over-emphasize this aspect when you do the book, as it's unusual. To see Oxford at her most typical, you want to be there in May and June, when the trees are all at the height of their beauty, and the water-meadows one solid sheet of golden buttercups, or, again, in autumn, when the trees are turning to red and gold, and the leaves beginning to flutter down. The underlying note of Oxford is her agelessness; she has grown old in body, but her spirit has never changed. It is her changelessness that is the key-note of Oxford."*

Again, William advised me to soak myself in the place and let Oxford speak to me. Well, I have been soaking *wet* many a time since I came to live here two years ago, yet I cannot remember how often Oxford and I have talked together!

The azaleas at Yatscombe, Boar's Hill, have also made friends for me. I have often attended lectures by Professor Gilbert Murray, and listened to him on the air taking part in the Brains Trust. He insists that the Chinese are a very polite people, and tells how once when he was attending a League of Nations Conference at Geneva, a Chinese delegate proposed a certain subject for discussion. The motion went through with only one dissentient vote, and that cast by the proposer himself who could not believe that the other delegates had upheld the motion for any other reason than charitable feeling. We have Professor Murray's word for the truth of this story. I would like to know who our delegate was. I cannot imagine that I would have done the same in his place!

Professor Gilbert Murray

Professor Murray, a very learned scholar, is modest and courteous. A familiar Chinese proverb says: "A great wiseman appears to know nothing." Professor Murray must be a great wiseman! His modesty broke down one day, however, when he was showing me the magnificent display of azaleas at Yatscombe, Boar's Hill. Their brilliant red, pink, yellow, and bronze seemed to fill the garden with flame, and quite out-dazzled the quieter charm of the rhododendrons. I saw the Professor's keen eye and happy smile as he contemplated his azaleas, ingeniously planted in a mass in the centre of a small dell rising into grassy slopes. Looking from the house situated farther up the main road to Boar's Hill, down to the valley, the masses of azaleas are like a huge cheerful fire warming the cold English spring. And why should Professor Murray not feel proud in possessing such a wonder in his own garden? He and Lady Murray have put up a notice "Please come in and look at the flowers", so that passers-by can share their pleasure. What an impressive and

Azalea

refreshing change from the eternal warnings to trespassers which abound in the English countryside!

The azalea, of which there are many species, is another flower which grows wild and freely on our hills and rocks. We call it "Cuckoo flower" because it blooms when the cuckoo begins to sing. I remember vividly, with a pang of nostalgia, the masses of azalea that in spring cover the hills outside my native city of Kiu-kiang, and how my cousins and I used in our childhood to pick huge armfuls of them, while as we picked the gaps seemed mysteriously to fill again. The azaleas at Yatscombe, though maybe not of the Chinese varieties, are dearer to me as I recollect the happy days of my childhood. Many of the great Chinese poets have been intoxicated by the beauty of this flower and have written an immense number of poems in praise of it. Perhaps they were attracted by the name "Cuckoo flower". A great T'ang poet, Po Chu-I, wrote:

Gently I break two small branches in my hand,
They do not look like flowers but fire-balls.

That is what it seems like to me. Every time I visited Yatscombe Lady Murray broke off an armful of azaleas for me to take home. I used to hold them as in days of old I would have held a flaming torch, and they would light up the whole 'bus and the passengers would turn and look. Such moments were proud ones for me.

There is a Chinese story about the azalea written some centuries ago. In the reign of T'ien-pao (742-755) of T'ang Dynasty there lived a hermit named Tsui Hsuan-wei who owned a big house in the eastern part of Lo-yang of Honan Province. He was a great believer in Taoism and ate many kinds of special herbs to keep himself young and healthy. After thirty years he exhausted the herbs he had collected, so he took his servants with him and went up into the Tsung mountains to collect more. In a year's time they returned to find the whole garden deserted and full of long grass and weeds. One spring night when the moon was bright and the wind clear and fresh, Tsui Hsuan-wei was alone in one of the courtyards undisturbed by his servants. After the third watch of the night there appeared a young maiden in blue who told him that she was going with a few friends of hers to visit an aunt at the upper eastern city-gate, and they would be glad of a rest there on their way. Tsui Hsuan-wei consenting, the girl went away and returned followed by three companions: one in green, introduced as Lady Yang, one as Lady Lee, one as Lady Tao; and the young girl in pink as Lady Shih O-tso. Each was accompanied by her personal maid. They all sat down together under the moon, and Tsui Hsuan-wei politely enquiring their plans, they answered that they wished to visit their eighteenth aunt, of the Feng family, for a few days. She had promised to visit them but had been unable to do so, so they were going to see her instead. Just at this moment Lady Feng was announced, and the ladies rose smilingly to welcome her. Lady Yang suggested that their host being very kind, they should stay here for a while. Tsui Hsuan-wei, who had politely withdrawn, came out again and was introduced to Lady Feng, to whom he bowed ceremoniously. He found her rather cold and aloof, and for some reason imagined her to be accustomed to woods and streams.

The ladies were all charming and beautiful, and a profusion of perfumes lingered in the air. Dinner was soon prepared and wine was brought. Each lady sang a song which Tsui Hsuan-wei tried hard to remember. First, the lady in red poured out some wine for the lady in white and then sang:

Pure and clear, your jade-like face
Looks more beautiful than the white snow
When you are gazing at the lovely moon.
Singing and sighing, you do not mean to complain about the spring wind.
I am only sad for myself at the thought that my youthful complexion will fade away.

Then the lady in white poured out some wine in turn and sang:

With red skirt gracefully and supply flowing like dew drops,
A slight touch of rouge adds charm to the beautiful flower.
You yourself may regret that you cannot keep your shy face for ever,
But please do not accuse the spring wind of deserting you!

When Lady Feng's turn came she held her wine-cup in such an unsteady manner that the wine upset on to Lady Shih O-tso's skirt. This unfortunate young lady flew into a rage and said to Lady Feng: "Everybody flatters you that you may not do them an injury, but *I* do not care!" And with these words she rose and left the party. Lady Feng, remarking sarcastically that she was merely showing off, also left, taking a southerly direction, while the others disappeared to the west. Tsui Hsuan-wei felt no strangeness in his experience.

The next evening the ladies came again. When they spoke of visiting Lady Feng, Lady Shih O-tso spoke angrily: "Why *should* we pander to that old woman? I wonder if Mr. Tsui would help us? My friends and I live in this garden," she continued, turning to her host. "Every year at the season of great winds our peaceful life is upset, and that is why we ask protection from Lady Feng. Her behaviour last night infuriated me, and we should do well not to see her again. If you are willing to give us protection you will be rewarded."—"What power have I to protect all you ladies?" asked Tsui. "If you will paint a red banner with the symbols of sun, moon, and five stars on it, and hang it on the top of a tall post erected in the eastern part of the garden, we shall all be spared from disaster. This year is already at an end, but on the morning of the twenty-first of the month there will be a gentle east wind, and if then you will do as I ask we shall be protected." Tsui Hsuan-wei agreed to help them, and they thanked him, promising always to remember his kindness. Then they went away, escorted to the end of the garden by Tsui Hsuan-wei.

In due course Tsui erected the post and hung the banner on it as he had been told. That morning there was a heavy east wind coming from Lo-yang and causing much havoc to the trees in its path, but the flowers in Tsui's garden still bloomed, untouched by its blast. Tsui Hsuan-wei awoke from his dream with the knowledge that his charming visitors had been goddesses of flowers, while Lady Feng was the goddess of the wind with power to control and distribute. Lady Yang was the goddess of the willow flower, Lady Lee of the apricot, Lady Tao of the peach blossom, and Lady Shih O-tso of the azaleas. A few nights later Tsui's visitors came again with a huge quantity of blossoms for him to eat which were supposed to have the effect of keeping him young and guaranteeing a very long life. It is said that Tsui Hsuan-wei was still alive in the beginning of the reign of Yuan-ho (806-820) and looked like a young man of thirty.

This story, probably written in the ninth or tenth century, has influenced the minds of our horticulturists for over a thousand years. In my younger days, as a boy of ten or so, I saw many a tall post bearing an exquisite red silk banner in the gardens of well-to-do families. I like a little fuss to be made of flowers. Is it not natural to make a fuss of those we love, even if only from superstition?

The petals of apricot and peach and other blossoms of the same kind are very delicate and have no resistance to wind, but azalea petals are stronger, and perhaps that is why the goddess of the azaleas would tolerate no nonsense from the goddess of the wind. Her subjects, despite the cold winds of an English spring, grow strongly and happily at Yatscombe, for Professor and Lady Murray have tended them carefully, planting them in the shelter of the valley. It is certainly not necessary to erect a banner-post at Yatscombe!

The magnolia has made me another friend in Oxford, Mr. Strickland Gibson, the keeper of the Bodleian Library.

I first came into contact with Mr. Gibson when I wrote seeking permission to use the Library, and during our correspondence he invited me to come and see his magnolia when next it was in bloom. I had no idea at that time whether I should still be in Oxford then, but I could not refuse an invitation so different from the usual formal invitations to dinner or tea to which I have become accustomed in England.

Meanwhile Mr. Gibson introduced me to the Bodleian. In the entrance hall he pointed out as items of particular interest the narrow, high-backed seats attached to the walls. In bygone days these had been the privileged seats of the library staff—and, indeed, he himself had used them some forty or fifty years ago—but were now no longer used. At the far end of Duke Humphrey's reading-room were similar seats, all elaborately carved, and some even with cushions—the privilege no doubt of professors and lecturers. It must have been most uncomfortable to sit up so straight and stiff, for any length of time. Perhaps this fact has at last been realized, for I have never myself seen any professor availing himself of a privileged seat. These seats reminded me of the cells into which Chinese candidates of ancient times were locked for three days while entering for the Imperial Civil Examination. It is strange that there have always been, and always will be, people eager for honour and privilege despite the discomforts attending their attainment. (Only recently I heard some one say what a privilege it was to live in this tragic but momentous age. I am afraid I do not appreciate that particular privilege!)

Eventually we found ourselves in the catalogue department, containing over one hundred and fifty large volumes. The Bodleian shares the privilege of the British Museum in receiving a copy of every book published in the British Isles, and its catalogue therefore increases rapidly. Mr. Gibson told me that just before the war the authorities were planning the reprinting of all the catalogues. This was to cost £10,000 and would take about fifteen years, but now it would take twenty years or more.

I have often read in the main building of the Bodleian, as well as the Radcliffe Camera, but my favourite haunt is among the tall old bookshelves in Duke Humphrey's reading-room.

I recently read an article called "We miss our Americans", by Mary Crosbie, which begins:

> *The Bodleian Library is one of the few places in Oxford where peace still seems to be. The city is full of exiles, and shops are thronged with hatless East Enders. But Bodley still houses books, not Government files. There you may find the even silence of the study, which is so unlike the breathing silence of a wood or a hill-top. Girls in red overalls have taken the place of the youths who formerly brought the books to your chosen table; but the older men, soft-voiced and remote, are there to advise and*

View of Oxford's towers and spires from a railway bridge near Lake Street

Autumn in Port Meadow

inform you. Untouched by war, I thought; and then suddenly I knew it was not—the silence was emptier.

And it ends: "Decidedly, we miss our Americans. After all, it's a new world we want to make." Miss Crosbie, no doubt, wrote this before American servicemen in their thousands flooded the streets and lanes of Oxford, but I do not think that Oxford has really missed the Americans for long, and now they have come, they wear uniform instead of civilian clothes. Often I have seen professors, chaplains and dons conducting uniformed Americans round the colleges, carefully explaining items of interest. This is a new job for them; but they have not interfered with the old Oxford guide, Mr. George Ray, who still seems very busy. John, the head porter at the Mitre Hotel, tells me that there is a constant stream of Americans coming and going. Oxford certainly cannot miss the Americans, but maybe it has grown tired of too many exiles and hatless "East Enders", and I, unfortunately, am both an exile and a hatless "East Ender"!

Time slipped by and soon it was spring again. A very small neat handwriting made its annual appearance in my letter-box: Mr. Gibson must have looked up his records and remembered that it was time to invite me to visit him again. This time I left my lodgings a little earlier and sauntered down the vast length of Morrell Avenue. The tall trees in the park were not yet in leaf, and the wide lawns were emerald green.

At the top of the avenue I paused to look at the magnificent pine trees standing regal and aloof in the middle of the road. I could philosophize for ever over a pine-tree.

Mr. and Mrs. Gibson greeted me at the door, while a bevy of charming young flower-faces peeped at me through the window, as though expecting me. Like many other youngsters born overseas, they were eager to meet one who had really come from their forefathers' birthplace. But they dared not anger their guardians, so they waited patiently, all cramped together, making a slight sound only when the gentle wind brushed by. Mr. Gibson introduced me.

The magnolia—a fair-sized tree—grew near the house, and with the soft green Hinksey Hills in the background made a most pleasing picture. When the glass doors were opened the charming young faces retreated hurriedly. Some were smiling broadly, some opened their tiny mouths as if about to speak, some were shy. They did not know what to ask first, so they stood there gazing at me and smiling. I too was speechless, lost in admiration of their dazzling beauty. I examined them closely and intimately. The inside of the six petals forming the flower was pure white, the outside was purple. They resembled somewhat the petals of a water-lily, though smaller. Chinese craftsmen have borrowed the shape and colouring of the magnolia petal in designing a certain porcelain spoon.

There were already a few petals lying on the ground, for the tree, Mr. Gibson told me, had been in bloom for several days. He had been busy lecturing at the college as well as carrying out his normal duties at the Bodleian, and had been unable to spend much time at home, and wanted now to enjoy his magnolia tree with me. A charming thought!

There are about eighteen or nineteen species of magnolia native to China. The Gibsons' tree I think is what we Chinese call a Mulan (wood-orchid), a tall, fine tree whose flowers have petals that are white inside and purple outside. If I am correct I should feel very close kinship, for its history is connected with my birthplace, Kiu-kiang. Kiu-kiang stands between Hankow and Shanghai, in the middle of the Yangtse river, which at this point is very wide. There used to be a small island here, called Mulan-chow on account of the large number of mulan trees which centuries ago grew on the Chow (island). I do not myself remember ever being on this island or ever seeing mulans there, but always in spring Kiu-kiang itself had many mulan trees, and it is no wonder that Mr. Gibson's magnolia gave me such joy.

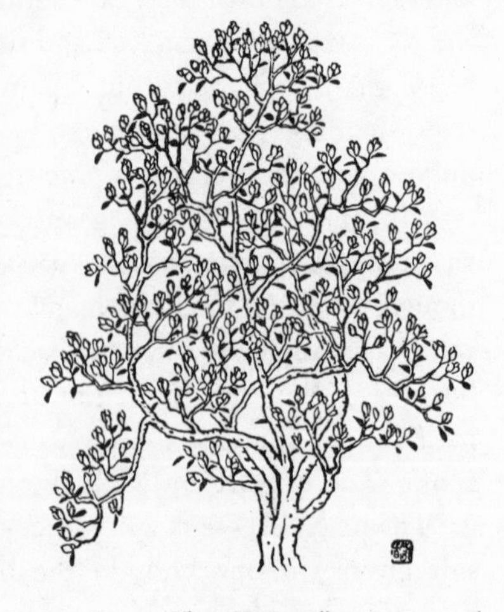
Gibson's magnolia

The magnolia is often called the crown prince among the more hardy plants. In China the species most admired is the Yulan, or jade-orchid. These trees often grow to more than a hundred feet in height; the majority vary between twenty and fifty feet. In full bloom, covered with white, lily-like flowers, this tree is like a jade screen or a small ornamental jade mountain. The flowers of this particular species, whose beauties have been sung by the great Chinese poets of all ages, possess a strong scent said to carry to a distance of two or three miles. The other day I happened to pick up an old English edition of a Shanghai newspaper and found a short description of the yulan orchid by an Englishman living in China.

> *Not all people [he said] like the trees, however; the fragrance is said to be too strong; this may be true; but the tree never looks better than when planted against a background of evergreens, and if they are kept away from the house, they are seen to the best advantage. If they are grown too close to windows, their delicious odour may be overpowering. The yulan (Magnolia denudata), or, as it is sometimes called, M. conspicua, has been cultivated for many centuries and it was used extensively for the embellishment of the garden of the Emperor of China. It figures often in Chinese poetry as a symbol of beauty and candour. The flowers are pure white in colour, and opening as they do on leafless branches so early in the year, they cannot help but attract our attention as we pass along the highways.*

I read also that about the year 1829 a Mr. Loudon mentioned having seen a tree of *Magnolia conspicua* in the Kensington Nursery, covered with eleven hundred tulip-like blossoms, snow-white and highly odoriferous. He considered it one of the finest specimens in the plant world, and observed that no person with the slightest pretensions to a love of plants, and a garden, should be without it. (Maund's *Botanic Garden.*) I wonder where this tree is now? Has it been destroyed, or moved away from Kensington owing to its strong scent? I myself love its scent, which I find much sweeter than that of the luxurious plants growing in big restaurants or the halls of lavish hotels.

To conclude this chapter I would like to relate a little story connected with a yulan. During the last year of my college life in Nanking I had a friend whose father, a famous literati, lived in large and beautiful old house in the southern part of this ancient city. My own home being far away, I was often invited to this house, and one day I received an invitation to an informal gathering of friends to celebrate the full-blooming of the yulans in the garden. Time in those carefree days was unimportant, and such a gathering would generally last the whole afternoon and evening. I arrived early, and when eight or nine guests joined us we all went into the garden. My friend, his young brother and myself were the only three young people there. Our elders in those days enforced their position of seniority very heavily. The existence of the younger generation was completely ignored, and we youngsters had to behave in a timid and subdued manner in accordance with the teaching of Confucius.

There were five yulans, all covered with white jade-like flowers and extremely beautiful. The elders shouted, laughed, joked, and sang, but the silence imposed on me gave me time to enjoy the magnolias. At about five o'clock hot rice-cakes, wine, dried-melon seeds, preserved lichih and lungyen, and green tea were served on the table in the middle of a small thatched bower. There were also papers, inks, brushes and books placed within easy reach. It was incredible what mess and noise those supposed-to-be-stern-faced elders made! After dark, dinner was laid on the table in a room facing the garden, where from the windows the masses of white blossom were visible. Eating and drinking went on interminably. Occasionally some one would get up and write a few lines and pass them to another guest to read; some one would sing, and laugh uproariously; another would draw a few strokes on a piece of paper, and another—and a third if necessary—finish the picture. A finished picture would provide a new subject of interest, and each would want to write a few words on it. It was fortunate that we youngsters had been trained on Confucian principles not to be gluttons, for otherwise there would have been nothing left for our elders to eat, although they had not come merely for the pleasure of eating and drinking.

I wonder why Confucious devoted so much of his philosophy to the benefit of the old and not the young? Perhaps it was because he began to expound his ideas when he himself was old. Had he been young when he formed his philosophy, he might have laid down a useful set of rules for the young. Now that I am middle-aged, of course I think highly of every word Confucius uttered in his "Analects"!

There came a time when our host, my friend's father, left the party, probably to go to his study. Reappearing suddenly, he urged us with a broad smile to gather round the dinner-table again, in the middle of which was set a large round dish of valuable porcelain. The lid was removed, and a warm gush of steam rose. We all dipped our chopsticks into the dish and brought out a delicately-flavoured morsel of food. Speculation arose as to the substance of the food, and our host eventually told us that he had been in the garden picking yulan petals. Coating them with a thin layer of batter he had fried them in deep cabbage-oil until they turned a crispy yellow. How delicious they were!—And what an imaginative and thrilling idea! We raised a hearty cheer, and several new poems were written in honour of this special dish (most of them rubbish, of course!). Some one declared that he had read about it in some book and was glad to have tasted a dish with such a wonderful flavour and texture. I too was glad. It was such an uncommon dish, more suited, perhaps, to the vegetarian. In all my forty years I have tasted it only this once, and I cannot help wondering if I shall taste it again. That beautiful house itself may not be in existence now after the ruthless bombing by the Japanese.

If ever I am fortunate enough to grow sufficient yulans to prepare this dish myself, I will certainly give the youngsters ample opportunity to express their opinion on it!

27
"When is a Rock not a Rock?"

"WHEN is a rock not a rock?"

"When it is a shamrock."

To me this trivial joke has a poetic ring. I repeated it one day to a friend of mine, Dr. Chang Lung-Yen, who had just flown over here from Berlin via Lisbon, China having declared war on Germany while he was an attaché in our Embassy there.

We were sitting in a corner of a small café called the "Shamrock", which stands opposite the University Students' Union in St. Michael Street. The "Shamrock" is noted for its home-made scones and cakes. I had been there for tea several times.

The café has an antique flavour of its own harmonizing with that of the rest of Oxford, but no one seems to know how it came into existence. I did learn, however, that the shamrock is the national emblem of Ireland. I noticed how the faces of some of my Irish friends lit up when I mentioned the shamrock to them—one was even inspired to sing "The Shamrock Leaf"!—and I wondered whether my face ever showed any change of expression when people mentioned winter-plum blossom or bamboo to me. I even went so far as to find out what a shamrock was like, how it grew, and where it could be found, until I had to laugh at myself for becoming like one of those amateur botanists or elderly English biologically-minded persons who delight in procuring exhaustive information about some tiny herb or weed. This was really not surprising, for I have been living amongst such people in Oxford.

My friend and I found it difficult to get a table in the "Shamrock" during the busy tea-hour. Both the room just above the main room and the top room were full, so we waited at the entrance in front of the cash-desk window, rather in the way of the harassed waitresses. This café always seems to be full. At last we found a table in a dark, cramped corner. I could just crane my neck sufficiently to look through the window at part of the Wesleyan Chapel tower in the distance, but I could not move my legs. I looked round at the wooden beams and whitewashed walls decorated with small pictures. Again I had the impression of great age, though actually the rooms do not look very old, and Dr. Chang refused to believe that they were. I begged that we should persuade ourselves of their antiquity and feel privileged to be there.

Dr. Chang and I were soon engaged in discussing poetry, and how the poetic mood was aroused by a poetic atmosphere. Dr. Chang is a good poet, and his inspiration flows so freely that he will compose a poem before he has finished one cup of tea. He now wrote down some of his own poems, and pointed out to me lines composed of very simple words so combined as to give a feeling of deep obscurity. "It is just this poignant feeling of obscurity or veiled meaning which makes a good line in a good poem," Dr. Chang continued, and he repeated a number of famous lines from the works of great Chinese poets which we both knew by heart.

I agreed with this statement. We were talking, of course, not about the principle of poetry, but about the technique of writing a good line so composed as to convey an impression that can be felt with the senses rather than understood by the intellect. This is the technique used in the Chinese classical style of poetry which has a precise number of words for each line and a precise rhyme and meter. Words are for use by every one, but the good poet will arrange them more skilfully than the bad. In Chinese poetry the allowance of words is very limited, and those poets who achieve an obscure meaning in a line, or in two or three lines, are considered the greatest poets.

But this is a vast subject. Dr. Chang agreed that the best poetry can only be felt, not understood. I mentioned that T. S. Eliot, in his essay on "Difficult Poetry", wrote: "I know that some of the poetry to which

I am most devoted is poetry which I did not understand at first reading; some is poetry which I am not sure I understand yet; for instance, Shakespeare's." I think T. S. Eliot would agree with us, though his subject is English poetry, which has a technique totally different from ours.

I remembered a little later that Desmond MacCarthy wrote about "The Poet and Humpty-Dumpty":

> *Of recent years a habit has grown upon many who write poetry and many who read it, of pretending that words have no central, hard core that cannot be dissolved by using them in particular contexts. "When I use a word," Humpty-Dumpty said in rather a scornful tone, "it means just what I choose it to mean—neither more nor less." Alice, you remember, doubted if it was possible to make words mean so many different things. "The question is," replied Humpty-Dumpty, "which is to be Master—that is all… Impenetrability! That's what I say," meaning by that word at that moment that he had had enough of the subject. Humpty-Dumptyisms are caricatures of the exquisite art of persuading words (and the same applies to images) to suggest things other than their primary meanings.*

I did not know, I said to Dr. Chang, whether I had thoroughly understood what Desmond MacCarthy meant, but this theory that words should not be persuaded to suggest things other than their primary meanings would not apply to the Chinese language. If it did,

Poetic mood

Chinese poets would have to invent a new vocabulary. We can permit ourselves to suggest a new meaning for a word if it gives a particular feeling in a particular context. Coleridge said: "Prose, words in their best order; Poetry, the best words in the best order." Words must be arranged beautifully and with painstaking precision.

Dr. Chang did not heed what I was driving at for he was deep in his own thoughts. He agreed, however, that "When is a rock not a rock," was very poetic, simply because this line had only the feeling, not the meaning. This abstract discussion brought inspiration to Dr. Chang, and he started to compose a new poem. Just then the following story came to my mind:

Poetic inspiration

> *The third and fourth of the unsuccessful candidates for the Newdigate Prize had a new field opened for their poetic talents about this time (1817) in the composition of the well-paid copies of verses (almost poems) with which not only the Lotteries and Potteries but even blacking-manufacturers and Jew tailors inundated the papers and covered the walls. "La! Sir," said the vulgar wife of a wealthy merchant of that stamp, "d'ye think we wastes our time in writing them stuffs and puffs? No, indeed, we keeps a poet from Oxford College."* [1]

This seemed to warn us not to try to write poetry in Oxford, since there must be many poets here, and we were in any case unlikely to acquire a similar occupation on account of our efforts as unsuccessful candidates for the Newdigate Prize.

On our way home we were preceded by an elderly couple. The lady was of considerable size, and walked in a heavy and stately manner with her chin up, while her husband, a very small and bashful creature, trotted along by her side like a child. They had evidently been shopping, and the husband bent forward to take the big paper carrier out of his wife's hand. It was a comical sight because he could not make her hand move at all.

When Dr. Chang suddenly murmured, "When is a rock not a rock?" I knew he was thinking of the large lady. It was only a poignant feeling, not comprehensible. We both laughed.

[1] Quoted from *Anatomy of Oxford.*

28
Friday the Thirteenth

HOW time flies! To me this metaphor, which to most people has come to seem so trite, is still expressive. Doubtless it arose in the days when flying, save for birds and angels, was as unthinkable as the invisible and intangible essence of time. One is aware of time only when it is gone. This fact has been brought home to me on several occasions lately by Rita, the little girl in the house where I live. She has been counting the days to her birthday. In two months, she keeps saying, she will be six years old, and when I first came to the house she used to say that she was "over three and a half ".

What have I learned about Oxford, I ask myself, during these two years while Rita has been growing from four to six? Of one thing, anyhow, I am positive: the times of the trains from Oxford to London and back: experience has engraved the hours on my mind.

While designing the décor and costumes for a Sadler's Wells ballet called *The Birds* I had frequently to travel up to London. There seemed perpetually to be some detail or other for which my attendance was required—some costumes had been finished and were to be fitted, or certain materials that I had chosen had proved unobtainable and others must be selected. And always the matter was urgent. No time to be lost.

Desiring one day (November 1942) to be in London by ten o'clock, I decided to catch the 8.05 train instead of the 8.40. It was a dark November morning which brightened as, with a feeling of rectitude due to the consciousness that I was catching an earlier train than was strictly necessary, I walked to the station. But on the platform confusion reigned. Impatient groups of people were demanding trains which were evidently not coming. No one seemed to know the cause of the breakdown. I was amused to see that some were quite unconcerned and strolled patiently up and down the platform. But others, like me, were puzzled. At 8.15 there was no sign of the 8.05.

At length we learned that there had been a smash overnight somewhere between Didcot and Oxford; and a little later those among us who were for Didcot and Reading were separated and put into a special 'bus. The rest of us allowed ourselves to be shepherded into a train of some kind which moved out almost at once.

There were six people in my compartment. One, a young lady, explained that she hoped to catch a train from Euston to Glasgow and asked what train she was in. No one knew. Another of the six, a soldier, said he was going to Princeton Borough. A third said *his* destination was High Wycombe. The young lady at once concluded that they were right and she wrong, and blamed the Oxford station-master for misdirecting her. But her irritation was soon forgotten. The war seems to have taught people patience. Presently the three were talking and joking together, and thereafter I was the only one anxious to discover the name of the stations at which the train stopped.

The 8.05, I knew, stops only at Didcot and Reading, and the 8.40 does not stop at all. But now we stopped at Cowley and other places whose names I knew only because during the blitz in 1940 I had travelled that way.

When my London flat was destroyed and I moved to Oxford, I had to go back to London every day or two on business, and usually I caught the 8.40—or what purported to be the 8.40, for its arrival and progress were unavoidably erratic. Crowds of business and professional people made for the same train, among them, I feel sure, many notable Oxford personalities whom I would like to have been able to identify. One I did know: Sir William Beveridge. He must have been on important government work then. Whenever I came on to the platform he was always there already. I had had two interviews with Sir William while I was doing some research work on English Local Government at the London School of Economics in 1934 and 1935, a study which I later

Punch and Beveridge

gave up. My first impression of Sir William has not been erased by the glare of publicity that has subsequently illuminated him. He reminded me forcibly of Mr. Punch: his prominent nose and long chin seemed unusually close together, forming a horse-shoe when seen in profile, and that means "luck" in this country. The upward curve of his wide mouth gave his face the effect of a permanent smile. Mr. Punch is always smiling and thousands of people smile back at him. To a Chinese—a foreigner—like me Sir William and Mr. Punch are both representative of England.

Once I found myself in the same compartment as Sir William. He was telling two friends that during the blitz he spent two nights in London every week. He slept in the basement of a large building and worked most of the night with no time to pay attention to bombs and A.A. guns. (How busy he has *always* been!) Presently he opened his leather case, took out his papers and worked until we reached Paddington. Then I understood why he had always been so anxious to get a seat on the train. I admire intensely the English democratic way of life that makes no special provision for a man like Sir William Beveridge who has to utilize every spare minute.

But I digress. We were at Princeton Borough. The soldier alighted. None of us knew what to do. The young lady wailed again, and was eventually instructed to change for the next fast train to London. She did so and the rest of us followed. An old lady in front of me kept murmuring: "Today is Friday the thirteenth—that's what it is." I had not realized this ominous fact. After an hour's wait, the old lady and I found ourselves in the same compartment of the next train, and she did not once stop saying: "Today is Friday the thirteenth..." I thought with wonder of the centuries through which primitive superstition has existed in the human mind. We may not be consciously superstitious, but almost any untoward event brings back our primitive notions. I did not suspect myself of being superstitious, but on hearing the old lady mutter, "Today is Friday the thirteenth," I said to myself, as though it explained everything: "So it is!" Then I smiled at myself.

I was not very late for my rendezvous, arriving just after twelve. Robert Helpmann was already there. This was the fourth or fifth time I had met him, and each time he reminded me of Eddie Cantor, the film star, by reason of his two big round eyes. Perhaps I should say that Eddie Cantor's eyes resemble Robert Helpmann's, but as I saw Eddie Cantor's film before I saw Robert Helpmann in the Sadler's Wells Ballet, I think of it as the other way round.

As I went into the room Helpmann was trying to put on his head the tail-piece of the male dove's costume, which was fan-like and looked, on him, like a Red-Indian's feathered head-dress. I watched his manner of walking with interest. It is a fascinating fact that one introduces unconsciously one's own professional manner or behaviour into one's private life, and this is particularly noticeable with Robert Helpmann, whose habit of swaying his body slightly from side to side is so slow and graceful. I remember that when we first met, at the Shanghai Restaurant, to discuss the décor and costumes for the "Bird" Ballet, he demonstrated to me, by movements of his fingers on the table, the steps of the dancers. I was vaguely reminded of Charlie Chaplin "dancing" with two rolls of bread on sticks in *The Gold Rush.* Suddenly he stretched out his right arm and leant forward against the table. His two big round eyes moved from end to end of the room as if viewing an audience, and he remarked humorously that the other diners must think him mad. I smiled. His eyes seemed to radiate sparkling and penetrating beams, and once I almost disbelieved him when he complained of being tired after travelling all night from Manchester to London, because his eyes were so wide-open and round.

Not long afterwards we were all gathered in the studio of Matilda Etches, who was responsible for the costumes, watching with interest the fitting of the male dove's costume on Alexis Rassine, whose rather

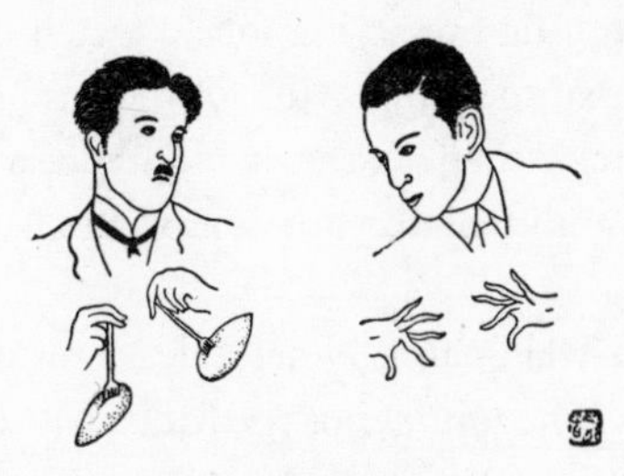

Chaplin and Helpmann

prominent nose indicates him for this dignified but melancholy character. Next came the fitting of the cuckoo costume on Gordon Hamilton, who is such a contrast to Alexis Rassine, and whose short stature and witty smiling face are so suited to his part. My design for the cuckoo was intended for a more bulky bird, but the costume was adapted to fit him perfectly. The varied colours suited him, and the white feather-like collar seemed to add length to his neck and the long tail to add to his stature.

In the afternoon Moyra Fraser and Beryl Grey came to be fitted for the costumes of hen and nightingale respectively. I had been anxious about the execution of the elaborate hen costume, for the hen is an important character in the ballet, and her costume had to be perfect in every detail. Very little had been accomplished at that time, but when I looked at the broad smile on Moyra Fraser's face and at her quickened humorous steps executed to see how the roughly-made part of the costume would fit the movements, I was confident that she would make the finished costume most attractive on the stage.

The nightingale costume, I must admit, was not very good in my original design. The nightingale, though singing beautifully at night, is a rather dull *looking* bird that has never earned distinction for the colour of its plumage. I had much difficulty in designing this costume and was really worried about it, for the nightingale's part is one of the biggest in the ballet, and my anxiety was heightened when I saw the elegant and lovely Beryl Grey, so full of youth and suppleness, and so perfectly suited, I was sure, although I had at that time never seen her dance, to her part. Happily, however, after much discussion and numerous suggestions from every one, the costume finally turned out to be very pretty.

It was an interesting but trying job to watch the fittings, especially after my journey that morning. Most of the costumes were unfinished, and I had to visualize them as they would appear when completed on the stage, which was difficult on account of the changes of colour caused by limelight.

Besides Robert Helpmann, Ninette de Valois was also there to help adjust each fitting. The founder of the Sadler's Wells Ballet, and its very busy director, she compelled my great admiration for the hard work she put in to make the new ballet successful. She even helped with the sewing of the costumes!

Matilda Etches showed great skill in executing the costumes and wonderful patience if any of us wanted to change a material or a colour. I am slow by nature, and my deliberate judgments must have worried her a good deal, but she showed no sign of it.

At half-past five every one had gone and I made ready to leave. When I picked up my overcoat from the floor I noticed the small piece of dark gold thread which was to be used for the trimming on the cuckoo costume. Matilda Etches was delighted to have found it, having searched for it all day. I repeated what the old lady in the train that morning had kept saying: "Today is Friday the thirteenth."—"So it is!" exclaimed Matilda Etches, tapping her head with her right hand and complaining that everything seemed to have gone wrong with her that day. We laughed about it together, and then I left.

Before catching the seven forty-five train for Oxford I had to see a friend near Belsize Park Road, and I had no time to get anything to eat. There were only two persons in the compartment with me, and at some station we had to change into a much fuller train. At Banbury we had to change into two more trains, and I have no idea how long we stayed there. More passengers remarked on this significant date, Friday the thirteenth, some grimacing, some laughing. After reaching Oxford I walked along the cold, dark, weary Walton Street, Kingston Road, and thence into Southmoor Road. These streets have become attractive to me on further acquaintance with Oxford, but that night they looked anything but attractive. I got home about three o'clock the next morning, which, thank goodness, was Saturday the fourteenth.

29
Not 'arf

MY motive in writing this book has been the humble one of describing my own insignificant perambulations round Oxford; and now I must come to an end. I remember reading that Mr. Geoffrey Parsons, one of the best known of American journalists, and chief editorial writer of the *New York Herald Tribune*, once said to an English writer: "It is a mistake to say that we talk the same language. The Yankee twang is as strange to English ears as the Oxford accent is to us. The real tie between our two countries is not a common tongue, but that we have the same ideas." Similarly, I am convinced that the tie between England and China, despite the difference in language, is similarity of ideas, and especially their respect for learning and their veneration of age.

Fellow-countrymen of mine who are lucky enough to visit the West are not considered really to have seen England if they have not paused, at any rate for one day, at Oxford. The Oxford recounted by these casual visitors can hardly be called adequate. The many Chinese studying in England are no doubt fully occupied with their studies, and few have the time to learn much of the life outside the institutions of learning they attend. I, on the other hand, have learned little of colleges, but I have been able to explore Oxford widely if not thoroughly. I know that many of my compatriots now in different parts of England are hoping, before returning to China, to visit Oxford, and I am sure that among the far greater number of young Chinese who will visit England after the war that desire will be even more widespread. I, having lived here for so long, will probably be asked for advice; so to save myself trouble, I propose to give prospective Chinese visitors a few hints here and now. I shall put down this information in the Chinese manner, the items all numbered "1" to signify that I place them all first and that I may add more at any time.

1. You may remember an old Chinese story about certain scholars. A tiger, after hunting in vain all day for food, returned to his den complaining loudly of hunger. The other tigers asked whether he had not met even a solitary man, and when he replied, "Yes, three, but I did not eat any of them," they were naturally curious to know why. So the tiger explained that the first man he met was a thin and dirty priest whom he considered quite unworthy of his stomach. Next he met a University graduate who had such a sour, pedantic flavour that he had to leave him. And the third man was a very musty and superannuated old boy, possibly a college don, but he could not possibly eat him in case he should break his teeth on such toughness. The moral of this is that in our country no priest can be rich, since the priesthood is not considered to be a profession, while scholars are generally poor because they do not know how to make money. Priests in Oxford live comfortably and wear beautiful long black gowns, and professors are given large rooms in the colleges and are quite well off. Since you are not a tiger, dear Compatriot, you need not hesitate to visit Oxford.

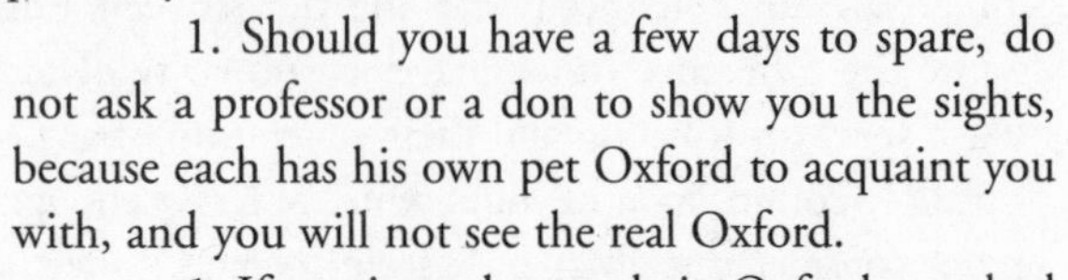

1. Should you have a few days to spare, do not ask a professor or a don to show you the sights, because each has his own pet Oxford to acquaint you with, and you will not see the real Oxford.

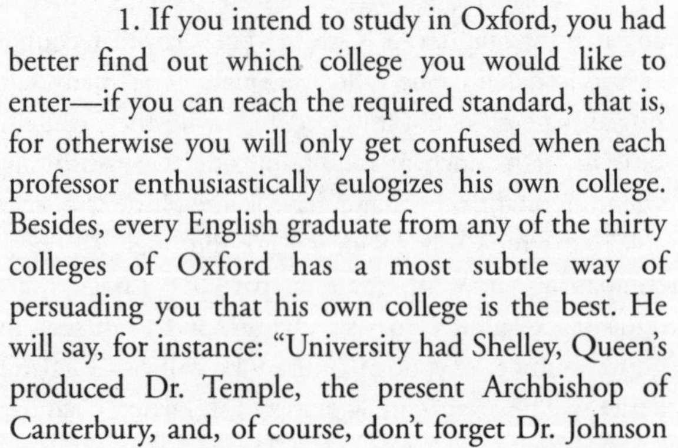

1. If you intend to study in Oxford, you had better find out which college you would like to enter—if you can reach the required standard, that is, for otherwise you will only get confused when each professor enthusiastically eulogizes his own college. Besides, every English graduate from any of the thirty colleges of Oxford has a most subtle way of persuading you that his own college is the best. He will say, for instance: "University had Shelley, Queen's produced Dr. Temple, the present Archbishop of Canterbury, and, of course, don't forget Dr. Johnson

Pembroke Gate

of Pembroke. But personally I prefer my own college, Oriel." After which you are still just as uncertain as ever. I may as well warn you now that no matter how much you may admire Trinity, you will be wasting your time in trying to enter it.

1. Make a point of seeing—and remembering—the four famous Oxford landmarks: Magdalen Tower, which might be compared to one of the square forts along our Great Wall; the Camera, like a reversed Pa-tou (a Chinese peck measure made of bamboo) with a small knob in the centre; St. Mary's Spire, like the top of a Tibetan Lama Pagoda with eight sides; and lastly, Tom Tower, a long tablet or monument on the back of a tortoise, but in round form. If you store these in your memory you can safely say that you know Oxford.

1. Take a ride on a Number 3 'bus to the terminus at Kingston Road, stand on the little bridge in Aristotle Lane, and pay homage to that great philosopher in the renowned city of learning.

Main gate of the front quad of Oriel College

1. Logic Lane in the High should not be missed, so that you can understand how sound is the logic of Oxford scholars who are convinced that what Oxford thinks must be right.

1. Stroll along Beef Hall Lane and Brewer Street, and you will realize that Oxford scholars are not so very different from ours in regard to eating and drinking. Each college, moreover, has a big kitchen of its own.

1. You should pay a visit to the Ashmolean Museum, where, in a small corner upstairs, an old cast-iron University Chest dated round about 1401 is on show. It was probably cast somewhere near the beginning of our Ming dynasty, so you can see how old Oxford is.

1. The little carvings of an elephant's head and of other animals under the windows on the outside wall of the Town Hall in St. Aldate's Street are worth close study. They are not very prominent, and you will be able to boast that you have seen something very special which it is

quite possible no one else has noticed for years. If you like, you can even write a beautiful essay to establish yourself as an authority on this particular subject.

1. You might try sitting on one of the seats near the City Library if you have an hour to spare, for assuredly, in due course, some of the older inhabitants of Oxford, dressed in Victorian fashion, with tall hats decked with a profusion of artificial flowers, will join you to gaze with the same interest as yourself at the other passers-by. And *then* you will be able to say that you have seen in person some of the typical English characters about which you have read in Charles Dickens.

Both Chinese and English scholars enjoy good food and wine

1. You should, if possible, make friends with an undergraduate and ask him to take you to one of the more popular pubs, so that you will understand in future what is meant by "the bulldog", the University Proctor, who stalks undergraduates frequenting pubs. If your undergraduate friend suddenly disappears from sight, you must not think him rude and unfriendly; and you need not feel too sorry for him, either, for he enjoys a game of hide-and-seek with "the bulldog".

1. If you can find the way to St. Helens Pass in New College Lane, a very narrow lane where there is room only for one person to squeeze through, you will find hidden away a Tavern which, it is alleged, undergraduates used at one time to climb the wall of a nearby college to visit without "the bulldog's" suspicions being aroused. Your imagination will be stirred by this recollection, and when you return to China you may even recommend similar devices for the convenience of Chinese undergraduates.

1. If you are in Oxford in the first term of the year, between say the end of October and the beginning of December, you should try to get into the gallery at the Students' Union in St. Michael Street during a debate. You need not actually listen, but it will amuse you to observe what keen interest and enthusiasm the youthful freshmen bring to the debate. Should one of the debaters be himself a freshman, you will have many a quiet chuckle as he imitates the manner and gestures of the better-known debaters, laying down the law in the most positive style. Later on in the university year, of course, when the freshmen are no longer "green", you will find it less amusing.

1. Should you be in Oxford during the second term of the university year, that is to say, in those incredibly cold months of January, February, and March, you might take a look at the rooms in the Union. This time you may not see many undergraduates, but you will be able, instead, to make a profitable study of the "old" Oxford men snoring round the big fire-places in the reading rooms, enjoying a peace which they declare they never get at home.

1. In case you can only come to Oxford in the third term, say between May or June, which is the time when visitors pour in, you will be better advised to learn something of the outside of Oxford, and to take a walk along any of the footpaths by the riverside. You need not squeeze yourself into the crowd to see the Eights (which you probably won't understand); you will get a decidedly more coherent idea of them from a good description by some famous Blue. You should instead walk slowly, or even sit on the grass by the river, to watch those clamorous undergraduates of both sexes rowing, swimming, gossiping and laughing together. Or you can find some quieter spot where you may chance to see a lonely boat lying idle on the opposite side of the river near a willow, with possibly a red, green or yellow parasol hiding its occupants from your sight and arousing your curiosity. But you must not be disappointed if your romantic interpretation is shattered and you see the parasol being closed to reveal an ancient couple, perhaps a man with a bald head and a lady with snow-white hair, both, maybe, bent with age. You may be momentarily startled, remembering that in China, in accordance with Confucius' teaching, our elders rarely show affection towards each other in public, particularly before young people, and that

Chinese ladies when once past their first youth will not wear very bright and startling colours. Should the old couple in due course pass close to you, would it not be a charming gesture to stand up and bow formally as we do to our elders at home? They may not understand your motive, but they will appreciate your courtesy.

1. I cannot imagine that any of you would attempt to write about the history of Oxford, but no doubt on your return you will wish to take steps to avoid the fact of your knowledge of Oxford and its position in the history of world civilization being overlooked. To be impressive you need not go to the Bodleian; you need not work under some well-known historian, for he will worry you to death with dates and incidents connected with Oxford. The best way is to make friends with some of the old college servants and ply them with drinks in the nearest pub. They will then become mellow and confidential and regale you with endless anecdotes of Oxford in bygone years. But be tactful and humble to them, for they have nearly all in their time served Lords, even Princes, as well as the sons and daughters of industrial magnates, and they are good judges of men.

1. It is unfortunate that it is hardly possible for you to see *all* the colleges, for you will undoubtedly be asked, after your visit, why there are thirty of them and not thirty-one or twenty-nine. The right answer to this question is that Oxford, or rather the British, want to keep their visitors, particularly the Americans, in the island as long as they can, and therefore they provide plenty of things to interest and amuse them.

1. When speaking to an Englishman, either in this country or in any other part of the world, it is vital that you should be very tactful in mentioning your visit, for you may not know at first whether he is an Oxford or a Cambridge man. You can easily discover this, however, by uttering the word "Oxford" slowly and distinctly. If he is an Oxford man his face will express emotion, while a "Cantab" will remain unmoved. If asked your opinion of the place, you need not say what you really think but just quote these sentences:

Wordsworth says:

Yet, O spires of Oxford! domes and towers! gardens and groves!

Lord Byron says:

What merry sounds proceed from Oxford bells.

De Quincy says:

Oxford, ancient mother! hoary with ancestral honours…

Thus you will always be on the safe side, for you will not have expressed your own opinion and cannot have excited the Oxford man or annoyed the Cambridge one.

1. Since it might one day be your lot to meet an Oxford man and a Cambridge man at the same time, you had better learn by heart this verse of Sir William Browne's:

The King to Oxford sent his troop of horse,
For Tories own no argument but force;
With equal care to Cambridge books he sent,
For Whigs allow no force but argument.

This will render all wangling between them impossible—except perhaps on the subject of your accent.

1. If you follow these instructions carefully you should be on firm ground. But should you find that the mention of Oxford annoys your companion, you may be sure he is a Cambridge man. You should then relate to him with all speed the familiar story that an Oxford and a Cambridge man were once arguing over the merits of their respective universities. They quarrelled over their colleges, their gardens, and everything else that *could* be quarrelled over. By way of clinching the argument the Cambridge man observed: "Well, anyway, we *reared* the Protestant Martyrs."—"Yes, I know," retorted the other, "and we burned them." So if you show that you prefer, after all, the humanity of Cambridge, the Cambridge fellow will be pleased with you.

1. Finally, your flat face will always identify you as an '"East Ender". You are sure to be asked, "How do you like Oxford?" and you will convince your interlocutor that he has placed you rightly by simply answering, "Not 'arf," which is equally appropriate from one who hails from the east end of the world as from the same part of London.